Adam Craig

**Room at the Top**

How to Reach Success, Happiness, Fame and Fortune

Adam Craig

**Room at the Top**
*How to Reach Success, Happiness, Fame and Fortune*

ISBN/EAN: 9783337340421

Printed in Europe, USA, Canada, Australia, Japan

Cover: Foto ©Suzi / pixelio.de

More available books at **www.hansebooks.com**

# ROOM AT THE TOP:

OR, HOW TO REACH

# Success, Happiness

## Fame and Fortune.

WITH BIOGRAPHICAL NOTICES OF SUCCESSFUL, SELF-MADE MEN,
WHO HAVE RISEN FROM OBSCURITY TO FAME, INCLUDING

GEN. JAS. A. GARFIELD,

ELIHU B. WASHBURNE,      DWIGHT L. MOODY.
CORNELIUS VANDERBILT,    GEORGE  PEABODY,
ROBERT FULTON,           ELIAS HOWE, Jr.,
HIRAM POWERS,            JAY GOULD,

THURLOW  WEED.

*WITH TEN PORTRAITS; ALSO RULES FOR BEHAVIOR
IN SOCIETY.*

BY A. CRAIG.

AUGUSTA, MAINE:
TRUE & CO.

# *PREFACE.*

**R**OOM AT THE TOP—always room there. Life has been likened to a ladder, the top round of which many people find it difficult to reach, some making but few steps upward, and others becoming disheartened when almost at the top.

The aim of this book is to set forth in plain, practical words, the best and truest course to pursue to reach the highest aims and end of life—SUCCESS, HAPPINESS, FAME AND FORTUNE.

To the young man starting out in life, who faithfully follows its teachings, it will act as a counselor, guide and friend.

The Biographical Sketches will show him what self-taught, hard-working, earnest men have accomplished, and act as an incentive to perseverance and determination in the effort to conquer all obstacles.

The RULE FOR BEHAVIOR will help him to acquire that gentlemanly deportment and politeness which tend to grace a man's intercourse with those with whom he is associated.

The selections have been culled from the works of well-known writers, whom opinions and authority upon such subjects are of great value and interest.

That many young men may find this little work of great service to them in their laudable efforts to succeed in life, is the sincere desire of

THE AUTHOR.

CHIGACO, 1882.

## PORTRAITS.

———

ELIHU B. WASHBURNE.

DWIGHT LYMAN MOODY.

GEORGE PEABODY.

CORNELIUS VANDERBILT.

ROBERT FULTON.

GEN. JAS. A. GARFIELD

ELIAS HOWE.

HIRAM POWERS.

JAY GOULD.

THURLOW WEED.

# CONTENTS.

————◆————

## WORK AWAY!

 ORK away!
  For the Master's eye is on us.
  Never off us, still upon us.
  Night and day!
  Work away!
Keep the busy fingers plying,
Keep the ceaseless shuttles flying;
See that never thread lie wrong;
Let not clash or clatter round us,
Sound of whirring wheels confound us;
Steady hand! let woof be strong
And firm, that has to last so long!
   Work away!

Bring your axes, woodmen true,
Smite the forest till the blue
Of Heaven's sunny eye looks through
Every wide and tangled glade;
Jungle swamp and thicket shade
   Give to-day!
O'er the torrent's fling your bridges,
Pioneers! Upon the ridges
Widen, smooth the rocky stair—
They that follow, far behind,

Coming after us, will find
Surer, easier, footing there ;
Heart to heart, and hand with hand,
From the dawn to dusk of day,
    Work away !
Scouts upon the mountain's peak—
Ye that see the Promised Land,
Hearten us ! for ye can speak
Of the country ye have scann'd,
    Far away !

    Work away !
For the Father's eye is on us,
Never off, still upon us,
    Night and day !
    WORK AND PRAY !
Pray ! and Work will be completer ,
Work ! and Prayer will be the sweeter ;
Love ! and Prayer and Work the fleeter
Will ascend upon their way !

Live in Future as in Present ;
Work for both while yet the day
Is our own ! for Lord and Peasant,
Long and bright as Summer's day,
Cometh, yet more sure, more pleasant,
Cometh soon our Holiday ;
    Work away !

—THE AUTHOR OF " THE PATIENCE OF HOPE."

# SUCCESS

### AND

# HAPPINESS.

# THE BEGINNING OF LIFE.

THERE is a charm in opening manhood which has commended itself to the imagination in every age. The undefined hopes and promises of the future—the dawning strength of intellect—the vigorous flow of passion—the very exchange of home ties and protected joys for free and manly pleasures, give to this period an interest and excitement unfelt, perhaps, at any other. It is the beginning of life in the sense of independent and self-supporting action. Hitherto life has been to boys, as to girls, a derivative and dependent existence—a sucker from the parent growth—a home discipline of authority and guidance and communicated impulse. But henceforth it is a transplanted growth of its own—a new and free power of activity, in which the mainspring is no longer authority or law from without, but principle or opinion from within. The shoot which has been nourished under the shelter of the parent stem, and bent according to its inclination, is transferred to the open world, where of its own impulse and character it must take root, and grow into strength, or sink into weakness and vice.

There is a natural pleasure in such a change. The sense of freedom is always joyful, at least at first. The mere consciousness of awakening powers and prospective work touches with elation the youthful breast.

But to every right-hearted youth this time must be also one of severe trial. Anxiety must greatly dash its pleasure. There must be regrets behind, and uncertainties before. The thought of home must excite a pang even in the first moments of freedom. Its glad shelter—its kindly guidance—its very restraints, how dear and tender must they seem in parting! How brightly must they shine in the retrospect as the youth turns from them to the hardened and unfamiliar face of the world! With what a sweet, sadly-cheering pathos must they linger in the memory! And then what chance and hazard is there in his newly-gotten freedom! What instincts of warning in its very novelty and dim inexperience. What possibilities of failure as well as of success in the unknown future as it stretches before him!

Serious thoughts like these more frequently underlie the careless neglect of youth than is supposed. They do not show themselves, or seldom do; but they work deeply and quietly. Even in the boy who seems all absorbed in amusement or tasks, there is frequently a secret life of intensely serious consciousness, which keeps questioning with itself as to the meaning of what is going on around him, and what may be before him—which projects itself into the future, and rehearses the responsibilities and ambitions of his career.

Certainly there is a grave importance as well as a pleasant charm in the beginning of life. There is awe as well as excitement in it, when rightly viewed. The possibilities that lie in it of noble or ignoble work—of happy self-sacrifice or ruinous self-indulgence—the capacities in the right use of which it may rise to heights of beautiful virtue, in the abuse of which it may sink to depths of debasing vice—make the crisis one of fear as well as of hope, of sadness as well as of joy. It is wistful as well as pleasing to think of the young passing year by year into the world, and engaging with its duties, its interests, and temptations. Of the throng that struggle at the gates of entrance, how many reach their anticipated goal? Carry the mind forward a few years, and some have climbed the hills of difficulty and gained the eminence on which they wished to stand—some, although they may not have done this, have yet kept their truth unhurt, their integrity unspoiled; but others have turned back, or have perished by the way, or fallen in weakness of will, no more to rise again.

As we place ourselves with the young at the opening gates of life, and think of the end from the beginning, it is a deep concern more than anything else that fills us. Words of earnest argument and warning counsel rather than of congratulation rise to our lips. The seriousness outweighs the pleasantness of the prospect.

---

## BEGIN WELL.

IT is a great point for young men to begin well; for it is in the beginning of life that that system of conduct is adopted, which soon assumes the force of Habit. Begin well, and the habit of doing well will become quite as easy as the habit of doing badly. " Well begun is half ended," says the proverb ; "and a good beginning is half the battle." Many promising young men have irretrievably injured themselves by a first false step at the commencement of life; while others, of much less promising talents, have succeeded simply by beginning well, and going onward. The good practical beginning is, to a certain extent, a pledge, a promise, and an assurance of the ultimate prosperous issue. There is many a poor creature, now crawling through life, miserable himself and the cause of sorrow to others, who might have lifted up his head and prospered, if, instead of merely satisfying himself with resolutions of well-doing, he had actually gone to work and made a good practical beginning.

Too many are, however, impatient of results. They are not satisfied to begin where their fathers did, but where they left off. They think to enjoy the fruits of industry without working for them. They cannot wait for the results of labor and application, but forestall them by too early indulgence.

---

## WHAT TO DO.

TO the young who stand, as it were, on the threshold of the great workhouse of the world, preparing to take their part in it, it becomes a serious and urgent consideration what part they are to take in it. After the formation of Christian principles, the choice of a profession is the most serious consideration that can engage their attention.

Perhaps the first step in the consideration is to realize the necessity of having definite work to do, and the real worth, and, if we may say so, sacredness of all honest work. There are few men who escape

the necessity of adopting some calling or profession;
and there are fewer still who, if they rightly understood their own interest and happiness, would ever
think of such an escape. For, according to that law
of work of which we have already spoken, life finds its
most enjoyable action in regular alternations of employment and leisure. Without employment it becomes a
tedium, and men are forced to *make work* for themselves. They turn their very pleasures into toil, and
undertake, from the mere want of something to do,
the most laborious and exhausting pastimes. To any
healthy nature, idleness is an intolerable burden; and
its enforced endurance a more painful penance than
the hardest labors.

It is not easy, however, for the young to realize
this. "Play" has been such a charm to their school-
boy fancy, that they sometimes dream that they would
like life to be all play. They are apt, at least, to take
to regular work with something of a grudge. They
have so many delays and difficulties about a profession,
that time passes on and they miss their opportunity.
There is no more serious calamity can happen to any
young man than this; and many a life has been wasted
from sheer incapacity of fixing on what to do. The
will gets feeble in the direction of self-denial of any
kind, and talents which might have carried their

possessor on to social consideration and usefulness, serve merely to illumine an aimless and pitied existence.

Young men who are, so to speak, born to work—to whom life leaves no chance of idleness—are perhaps the most fortunate. They take up the yoke in their youth. They set their faces to duty from the first; and if life should prove a burden, their backs become inured to it, so that they bear the weight more easily than others do pleasures and vanities. In our modern life, this is a largely-increasing class. As the relations of society become more complicated, and its needs more enlarged, refined, and expensive, the duty of work—of every man to his own work—becomes more urgent and universal. There is no room left for the idle. There are certainly no rewards to them. Society expects every man to do his duty; and its revenge is very swift when its claims are neglected or its expectations disappointed.

But it is at least equally important for young men to begin life with an intelligent appreciation of work as a whole, and to free their mind from the prejudices which have so long prevailed on this subject. It is singular how long and to what extent these prejudices have prevailed. Some kinds of employment have been deemed by traditionary opinion to be honorable, and such as gentlemen may engage in; others have been deemed to be base, and unfit for gentlemen. Why so? It would puzzle any moralist to tell. The profession of a soldier is supposed to be the peculiar profession of a gentleman; that of a tailor is the opprobrium of boys and the ridicule of small wits. Is there not something untrue as well as unworthy in the implied comparison?

Let young men, and young women too, of whatever grade of life, to whom there may seem no opening in the now recognized channels of professional or domestic activity which have been conventionally associated with their position, make to themselves, as they may be able, an opening in the ranks of commercial or mechanical employment. If society, from its very increase of wealth and refinement, and the expensive habits which necessarily flow from this increase, creates obstacles to an advantageous settlement in life after the old easy manner to many among the young, it certainly ought not by its prejudices to stand in the way of their launching upon the great world of life in their own behalf, and attaining to what industrial independence and prosperity they can.

It is at least a right and wise feeling for the young to cultivate—that there is no form of honest work which is really beneath them. It may or may not be

suitable for them.   It may or may not be the species
of work to which they have any call.   But let them
not despise it.   The grocer is equally honorable with
the lawyer, and the tailor with the soldier, as we have
already said.   It is just as really becoming a gentleman—if we could purge our minds of traditional delu-
sions which will not stand a moment's impartial
examination—to serve behind a counter as to sit at a
desk, to pursue a handicraft as to indite a law paper
or write an article.   The only work that is *more honorable*, is work of higher skill and more meritorious excellence.   It is the qualities of the workman, and not
the name or nature of the work, that is the source of
all real honor and respect.—*Tulloch.*

---

## WHAT AM I FIT FOR ?

THE professions to which life invites the young
are of very various kinds ; and the question of
choice among them, as it is very important, is
sometimes also very trying and difficult. Rightly viewed,
it ought to be a question simply of capacity.   What
am I fit for?   But it is more easy in many cases to ask
this question than to answer it.   It will certainly, however, facilitate an answer, to disembarrass the mind of

such prejudices as we have been speaking of. The
field of choice is in this manner left comparatively
open.   Work as such, if it be honest work, is esteemed
not for the adventitious associations that may surround
it, but because it offers an appropriate exercise for
such powers as we possess, and a means of self-sup-
port and independence.

There are those to whom the choice of a profession
presents comparatively few difficulties.   They are
gifted with an aptitude for some particular calling, in
such a degree that they themselves and their friends
discern their bent from early youth, and they grow up
with no other desire than to betake themselves to
what is acknowledged to be their destiny in the world.
Such cases are, perhaps, the happiest of all , but they
are far from numerous.   A special aptitude is seldom
so prononnced in youth.   Even where it exists, it lies
hid many a time, and unknown even to its possessor,
till opportunity calls it forth.

There are other cases where the circumstances of
the young are such as to mark out for them, without
deliberation on their part, the profession which they
are to follow.   Family traditions and social advantages may so clearly point their way in life that they
never hesitate.   They have never been accustomed
to look in any other direction, and they take to their

lot with a happy pride, or at least a cheerful contentment.

But the great majority of young men are not to be found in either of these envied positions. They have their way to make in the world; and they are neither so specially gifted, on the one hand, nor so fortunately circumstanced, on the other eand, as to see clearly and without deliberation the direction in which they should turn, and the fitting work which they should give themselves.

Many things must be considered by them and for them in such a case which we are not called upon to discuss here—which, indeed, we cannot discuss here. The accidents of position, with which, after all, the balance of their lot may lie, vary so indefinitely that it would be impossible to indicate any clear line of direction for them. But without venturing to do this, it may be useful to fix the thoughts of the young upon certain general features of the various classes of professions that lie before them in the world open for their ambition and attainment.

Professions may be generally classified as intellectual, commercial, and mechanical, excluding those which belong to the public service, such as the army and navy, and the civil offices under Government. These form by themselves a class of professions of great importance.   But the aptitudes which they require are, upon the whole, less determined, and therefore less easily characterized than those which the ordinary professions demand.   A merchant or a shoemaker, or even a clergyman, may become, should circumstances summon him, a soldier or a diplomatist, but neither the soldier nor diplomatist could so easily assume the functions of the merchant, or shoemaker, or clergyman.

Neither must it be supposed, in making this classification, that the names we have used have anything more than a general application warranted by the talk of society, and, therefore, sufficiently intelligible. There are certain callings which society has agreed to consider more intellectual, more of the character of professions, and others which it regards as more peculiarly of a business or commercial character, and others again that are more of the nature of a craft, or handiwork.   In point of fact, all are intellectual in the sense of calling into exercise the intellectual powers; and it may so happen that more mental capacity may be shown in conducting affairs of business, or in inventing or applying some new mechanical agency, than in the discharge of the duties of the intellectual professions, commonly so called.   This does not, however, affect the propriety of the classification.   The subject-matter of the callings is nevertheless distinct. Those of the first class deal more largely and directly with the intellectual nature of man; they involve a more special mental training; while those of the other two classes deal more with the outward industrial activities, and are presumed not to require so prolonged or careful an intellectual education.

This obvious distinction serves to mark generally the qualities that are demanded in these respective orders of professions. Whether a man is to be a clergyman, lawyer (using the word in its largest sense as including the profession of the bar), physician—or a merchant, an engineer, or an ordinary tradesman, should depend, in a general way at least, on the comparative vivacity and force of his intellectual powers. A youth who has but little intellectual interest, who cares but little or not at all for literary study and the delights of scholastic ambition, is shut out by nature from approach to the former professions. They are not *his* calling in any high or even useful sense. He may approach them and enter upon them, and a certain worldly success may even await him in them under the favoring gale of circumstances; but according to any real standard of excellence or utility, he has missed his proper course in life. He may have found what he wanted, but others will often have failed to find in him what they were entitled to expect.

The same is no less true of the Bar or legal profession in all its bearings and of the profession of Medicine. Each of these professions demand a vivacious intellectual interest, powers of real and independent thought. Neither their principles can be grasped, nor their highest applications to the well-being of society appreciated, without these. All, it may be said, are not required to rise so high ; there must be common as well as higher workmen in all professions—"hewers of wood and drawers of water," as well as men of wide and commanding intelligence. And this is true. Only the question remains, whether those who never rise above the mechanical routine of the higher professions would not have been really more happy and useful in some lower department of industry. In contemplating a profession none should willingly set before them the prospect of being nothing but a Gideonite in it. And yet this must be the fate, and deserves to be the fate, of all who rush towards work for which nature has given them no special capacity. By aiming beyond their power, they are likely to fall short of the competency and success that, in some more congenial form of work, might have awaited them.

It seems so far, therefore, that there is a sufficiently plain line of guidance as to the choice of a profession. If your interest is not in study, if your bent is not intellectual, then there is one large class of professions for which *you* are not destined. You may be intellectual, highly so, and yet you may not choose any of these professions; circumstances may render this inadvantageous ; or, while your intellectual life is inquisitive and powerful, your active ambition may be no less powerful, and may carry you away. But at any rate, if you have not a lively interest in intellectual pursuits, neither the Church, nor the Bar, nor Medicine is your appropriate professional sphere. You can never be in any of these a "workman needing not to be ashamed."

Nor let it be supposed that there is anything derogatory in this lack of intellectual interest in the sense in which we now mean. It by no means implies intellectual ignorance or indisposition to knowledge, but simply no predominating desire for study as a habit and mode of life. It is not the book in the quiet room that interests you so much as the busy ways of the world, the commercial intercourse of men, or, it may be, some mechanical craft to which your thoughts are ever turning, and your hands inclining. How constantly are such differences observed in boys! Schol-

astic tastes weary and stupefy some who are all alert
as soon as the unwelcome pressure is lifted from their
minds, and their energies are allowed their natural
play. Their aptitude is not for classic lore; their
delight is not in lore at all, but in active work of some
kind, the interest of which is of an every-day practical
character.

The simple rule in such a case is—follow your bent.
It may not show itself so particularly as in some cases
we have already supposed; but, at least, it is so far
manifest. It is clearly not in certain directions, and
so far, therefore, the field of your choice is limited.
Probe a little deeper and more carefully, and it may
come more plainly into view. And, remember, one
bent is really as honorable as another, although it may
not aim so high. The young merchant is just as
clearly "called" as the young clergyman, if he feel
the faculty of business stirring in him. And who seem
often more called than great mechanicians—men often
with little general knowledge, and little intellectual
taste and sympathy, but who have a creative faculty of
designs, as determinate in its way as the art of the
painter or the poet?

These are special cases. But in ordinary youth
something of the same kind may be observed. There
are boys designed by nature for commercial life; there

are others plainly designed for mechanical employment. Nature has stamped their destiny upon them in signs which show themselves, if sought after. Let not them and their friends try to countersign the seal of nature. This is always a grievous harm ; a harm to the individual, and a possible harm to the world.

Even where Nature's indications may be obscure, there seems no other rule than to trace and follow them. Some boys of healthy and well-developed faculties, or, still more likely, of weak and unemphatic qualities, may seem to have no particular destiny in the world. Yet they have. Their place is prepared for them, if they can find it. And their only hope of doing so is to observe nature, and follow it. She may not have written her lines broadly on their souls, but she has put tracings there, which may be found and followed. There are a few who may seem to find their position in the world more by accident than anything else. Circumstances determine their lot, and without any thought of theirs, they seem to get into the place most fitting them. Yet even in such cases, circumstances are often less powerful than are supposed, or, at least, they have wrought with nature, and this unconscious conformity has proved the strongest influence in fashioning such lives to prosperity and success.

For strong natures there is strong work; for weak
and less certain natures, there is also work, but not of
the same kind.   The back is fitted to the burden in a
higher sense than is sometimes meant, if only the
back do not overtask its powers, and assume to carry
weight that was never meant for it.—*Tulloch.*

------

## RESISTANCE TO TEMPTATION.

THE young man, as he passes through life, advances    through   a   long   line   of   tempters
ranged   on   either   side   of   him; and the inevitable effect of yielding is degradation in a greater
or less degree.   Contact with them tends insensibly
to draw away from him some portion of the divine
electric element with which his nature is charged;
and his only mode of resisting them is to utter and
to act out his "No" manfully and resolutely.   He
must decide at once, not waiting to deliberate and
balance reasons; for the youth, like "the woman who
deliberates, is lost."   Many deliberate, without decid-
ing, but "not to resolve, *is* to resolve."   A perfect
knowledge of man is in the prayer, "Lead us not into
temptation."   But temptation will come to try the
young man's strength; and once yielded to, the power

to resist grows weaker and weaker. Yield once, and a portion of virtue has gone. Resist manfully, and the first decision will give strength for life; repeated, it will become a habit. It is in the outworks of the habits formed in early life that the real strength of the defence must lie; for it has been wisely ordained, that the machinery of moral existence should be carried on principally through the medium of the habits, so as to save the wear and tear of the great principles within. It is good habits which insinuate themselves into the thousand inconsiderable acts of life, that really constitute by far the greater part of man's moral conduct.

Hugh Miller has told how, by an act of youthful decision, he saved himself from one of the strong temptations so peculiar to a life of toil. When employed as a mason, it was usual for his fellow-workmen to have an occasional treat of drink, and one day two glasses of whiskey fell to his share, which he swallowed. When he reached home, he found, on opening his favorite book—"Bacon's Essays"—that the letters danced before his eyes, and that he could no longer master the sense. "The condition," he says, "into which I had brought myself was, I felt, one of degradation. I had sunk, by my own act, for the time, to a lower level of intelligence than that on which it was my privilege to be placed; and though the state could have been no very favorable one for forming a resolution, I in that hour determined that I should never again sacrifice my capacity of intellectual enjoyment to a drinking usage; and with God's help, I was enabled to hold by the determination." It is such decisions as this that often form the turning-points in a man's life, and furnish the foundation of his future character. And this rock, on which Hugh Miller might have been wrecked, if he had not at the right moment put forth his moral strength to strike away from it, is one that youth and manhood alike need to be constantly on their guard against. It is about one of the worst and most deadly, as well as extravagant, temptations which lie in the way of youth. Sir Walter Scott used to say "that of all vices, drinking is the most incompatible with greatness." Not only so, but it is incompatible with economy, decency, health, and honest living. When a youth cannot restrain, he must abstain. Dr. Johnson's case is the case of many. He said, referring to his own habits, "Sir, I can abstain; but I can't be moderate."—*Smiles.*

———

Here are Dr. Thomas Guthrie's excellent reasons for becoming a total abstainer: "I have tried both ways; I speak from experience. I am in good spirits because I take no spirits; I am hale because I use no ale; I take no antidote in the form of drugs because I take no poison in the form of drinks. Thus, though in the first instance I sought only the public good, I have found my own also since I became a total abstainer. I have these four reasons for continuing to be one: first, my health is stronger; second, my head is clearer; third, my heart is lighter; fourth, my purse is heavier."

In the course of a recent address at Exeter Hall, London, Mr. John B. Gough said: " I knew a man in America who undertook to give up the habit of chewing tobacco. He put his hand in his pocket, took out his plug of tobacco and threw it away, saying as he did so, 'That's the end of it.' But it was the beginning of it. Oh, how he did want it! He would lick his lips, he would chew camomile, he would chew toothpicks, quills—anything to keep the jaws going. No use; he suffered intensely. After enduring the craving for thirty-six or forty-eight hours, he made up his mind, 'Now, it's no use suffering for a bit of tobacco; I will go and get some.' So he went and purchased another plug, and put it in his pocket. 'Now,' he said, 'when I want it awfully, I'll take some.' Well, he did want it awfully; and he said he believed that it was God's good Spirit that was striving with

3

him as he held the tobacco in his hand. Looking at it, he said, 'I love you. But are *you* my master, or am I yours? You are a *weed*, and I am a *man*. You are a *thing*, and I am a *man*. I'll master you, if I die for it.' Every time he wanted it he would take it out and talk to it. It was six or eight weeks before he could throw it away and feel easy ; but he said the glory of the victory repaid for all his struggle."

## A HIGH STANDARD NECESSARY.

BUT to wrestle vigorously and successfully with any vicious habit, we must not merely be satisfied with contending on the low ground of worldly prudence, though that is of use, but take stand upon a higher moral elevation. Mechanical aids, such as pledges, may be of service to some, but the great thing is to set up a high standard of thinking and acting, and endeavor to strengthen and purify the principles, as well as to reform the habits. For this purpose a youth must study himself, watch his steps, and compare his thoughts and acts with his rule. The more knowledge of himself he gains, the more humble will he be, and perhaps the less confident in his own strength. But the discipline will be found most valuable which is acquired by resisting small present gratifications to secure a prospective greater and higher one.   It is the noblest work in self-education—for

> " Real glory
> Springs from the silent conquest of ourselves,
> And without that the conqueror is nought
> But the first slave."
>
> —*Smiles.*

## ALL HONEST INDUSTRY HONORABLE.

**T**HERE is no discredit, but honor, in every right walk of industry, whether it be in tilling the ground, making tools, weaving fabrics, or selling the products behind a counter. A youth may handle a yard-stick, or measure a piece of ribbon ; and there will be no discredit in doing so, unless he allows his mind to have no higher range than the stick and ribbon ; to be as short as the one, and as narrow as the other.  " Let not those blush who *have*," said Fuller, " but those who *have not* a lawful calling." And Bishop Hall said, " Sweet is the destiny of all trades, whether of the brow or of the mind."   Men who have raised themselves from a humble calling, need not be ashamed, but rather ought to be proud of the difficulties they have surmounted.  The laborer

on his feet stands higher than the nobleman on his
knees. One of our Presidents, when asked what was
his coat-of-arms, remembering that he had been a
hewer of wood in his youth, replied, " A pair of shirt-
sleeves." Lord Tenterden was proud to point out to
his son the shop in which his father had shaved for a
penny. A French doctor once taunted Flechier,
Bishop of Nismes, who had been a tallow-chandler in
his youth, with the meanness of his origin, to which
Flechier replied, " If you had been born in the same
condition that I was, you would still have been but a
maker of candles." Some small spirits, ashamed of
their origin, are always striving to conceal it, and by
the very efforts they make to do so, betray themselves;
like that worthy but stupid Yorkshire dyer, who, having gained his money by honest chimney-sweeping,
and feeling ashamed of chimneys, built his house
without one, sending all his smoke into the shaft of his
dye-works.—*Smiles.*

## *MONEY-MAKING.*

**M**ANY popular books have been written for the
purpose of communicating to the public the
grand secret of making money. But there
is no secret whatever about it, as the proverbs of every

nation abundantly testify. "Many a little makes a meikle."

"Take care of the pennies and the pounds will take care of themselves."

"A penny saved is a penny gained."

"Diligence is the mother of good-luck."

"No pains no gains."

"No sweat no sweet."

"Sloth, the key of poverty."

"Work, and thou shalt have."

"He who will not work, neither shall he eat."

"The world is his, who has patience and industry."

"It is too late to spare when all is spent."

"Better go to bed supperless than rise in debt."

"The morning hour has gold in its mouth."

"Credit keeps the crown of the causeway."

Such are specimens of the proverbial philosophy, embodying the hoarded experience of many generations, as to the best means of thriving in the world. They were current in people's mouths long before books were invented; and, like other popular proverbs, they were the first codes of popular morals. Moreover, they have stood the test of time, and the experience of every day still bears witness to their accuracy, force and soundness.

The proverbs of Solomon are full of wisdom, as to

the force of industry, and the use and abuse of money: " He that is slothful in work is brother to him that is a great waster." " Go to the ant, thou sluggard; consider her ways and be wise." Poverty, he says, shall come upon the idler, " as one that traveleth, and want as an armed man; " but of the industrious and upright, "The hand of the diligent maketh rich." " He who will not plough by reason of the cold, shall beg in harvest, and have nothing." " The drunkard and the glutton shall come to poverty; and drowsiness shall clothe a man with rags." " The slothful man says there is a lion in the streets." " Seest thou a man diligent in his business? he shall stand before kings." But above all " It is better to get wisdom than gold; for wisdom is better than rubies, and all the things that may be desired are not to be compared to it."

Simple industry and thrift will go far towards making any person of ordinary working faculty comparatively independent in his means. Even a working man may be so, provided he will carefully husband his resources and watch the little outlets of useless expenditure.

Nothing, however, is more common than energy in money-making, quite independent of any higher object than its accumulation. A man who devotes himself to this pursuit, body and soul, can scarcely fail to become rich. Very little brains will do; spend less than you earn; add dollar to dollar; scrape and save; and the pile of gold will gradually rise. John Foster quoted a striking illustration of what this kind of determination will do in money-making. A young man who ran through his patrimony, spending it in profligacy, was at length reduced to utter want and despair. He rushed out of his house, intending to put an end to his life, and stopped on arriving at an eminence overlooking what were once his estates. He sat down, ruminated for a time, and rose with the determination that he would recover them. He returned to the streets, saw a load of coals which had been shot out of a cart on to the pavement before a house, offered to carry them in, and was employed. He thus earned a few pence, requested some meat and drink as a gratuity, which was given him, and the pennies were laid by. Pursuing this menial labor, he earned and saved more pennies; accumulated sufficient to enable him to purchase some cattle, the value of which he understood, and these he sold to advantage. He now pursued money with a step as steady as time, and an appetite as keen as death ; advancing by degrees into larger and larger transactions, until at length he became rich. The result was, that he more than recovered his possessions, and died an inveterate miser. When he was buried, mere earth went to earth. With a nobler spirit, the same determination might have enabled such a man to be a benefactor to others as well as to himself. But the life and its end in this case were alike sordid.—*Smiles.*

---

## THE LOVE OF MONEY.

THE saving of money for the mere sake of it, is but a mean thing, even though earned by honest work ; but where earned by dice-throwing, or speculation, and without labor, it is still worse. To provide for others, and for our own comfort and independence in old age, is honorable, and greatly to be commended ; but to hoard for mere wealth's sake is the characteristic of the narrow-souled and the miserly.· It is against the growth of this habit of inordinate saving, that the wise man needs most carefully to guard himself ; else, what in youth was simple economy, may in old age grow into avarice, and what was a duty in the one, may become a vice in the other. It is the *love* of money—not money itself —which is the "root of evil"—a love which narrows and contracts the soul, and closes it against generous life and action. Hence, Sir Walter Scott makes one of his characters declare that " the penny siller slew mair souls than the naked sword slew bodies." It is one of the defects of business too exclusively followed, that it insensibly tends to a mechanism of character. The business man gets into a rut, and often does not look beyond it. If he lives for himself only, he becomes apt to regard other human beings only in so far as they minister to his ends. Take a leaf from such men's ledger, and you have their life. It is said of one of our most eminent modern men of business— withal a scrupulously honorable man—who spent his life mainly in money-making, and succeeded, that when upon his death-bed, he turned to his favorite daughter, and said solemnly to her, " Hasn't it been a mistake, —— ? " He had been thinking of the good which other men of his race had done, and which he might have done, had he not unhappily found exclusive money-making to be a mistake when it was too late to remedy it.—*Smiles.*

———

## *RICHES NO PROOF OF WORTH.*

ORLDLY success, measured by the accumulation of money, is no doubt a very dazzling thing ; and all men are naturally more or less the admirers of worldly success. But though men of persevering, sharp, dexterous, and unscrupulous habits, ever on the watch to push opportunities, may and do " get on " in the world ; yet it is quite possible that they may not possess the slightest elevation of character, nor a particle of real greatness. He who recognizes no higher logic than that of the dollar, may become a very rich man, and yet remain áll the while an exceedingly poor creature. For riches are no proof whatever of moral worth ; and their glitter often serves only to draw attention to the worthlessness of their possessor, as the glowworm's light reveals the grub. " In morals," says Mr. Lynch, " a penny may outweigh a pound—may represent more industry and character. The money that witnesses of patient, inventive years of fair dealing and brave dealing, proves 'worth' indeed. But neither a man's means nor his worth are measurable by his money. If he has a fat purse and a lean heart, a broad estate and a narrow understanding, what will his ' means ' do for him—what will his 'worth' gain him ? " Let a man be what he will, it is the mind and heart that make a man poor or rich, miserable or happy; for these are always stronger than fortune.

The manner in which so many allow themselves to be sacrificed to their love of wealth, reminds one of the cupidity of the monkey—that caricature of our species. In Algiers, the Kabyle peasant attaches a gourd, well fixed, to a tree, and places within it some rice. The gourd has an opening merely sufficient to admit the monkey's paw. The creature comes to the tree by night, inserts his paw, and grasps his booty. He tries to draw it back, but it is clenched, and he has not the wisdom to unclench it. So there he stands till morning, when he is caught, looking as foolish as may be, though with the prize in his grasp. The moral of this little story is capable of a very extensive application in life.—*Smiles.*

## *EVILS OF SELF-INDULGENCE.*

IF, like Cleopatra, you had dissolved a pearl—if you had put together the income of years—all that has been spent on self-indulgence—perhaps in enticing others into sin—could you have put it all together, and, like the queenly jewel, dissipated it in dust and air, we might have been sorry for the idle sacrifice, but the wasted money would not have wasted you. Cleopatra had another pearl, the gift of peerless beauty. That gift was perverted, and it hatched a serpent; it came back into her bosom—the asp which stung her. So with the possessions of the prodigal.

Talents laid up in a napkin, pearls melted in vinegar, will benefit no one; but rank, fortune, health, high spirits, laid out in the service of sin, are scorpion-eggs, and fostered and fully grown, the forthcoming furies will seize on the conscience, and with stings of fire will torment it evermore.—*Hamilton.*

## POWER OF MONEY OVER-ESTIMATED.

THE power of money is, on the whole, over-estimated. The greatest things which have been done for the world have not been accomplished by rich men, or by subscription lists, but by men generally of small pecuniary means. Christianity was propagated over half the world by men of the poorest class; and the greatest thinkers, discoverers, inventors, and artists, have been men of moderate wealth, many of them little raised above the condition of manual laborers in point of worldly circumstances. And it will always be so. Riches are oftener an impediment than a stimulus to action; and in many cases they are quite as much a misfortune as a blessing. The youth who inherits wealth, is apt to have life made too easy for him, and he soon grows sated with it, because he has nothing left to desire. Having no special object to struggle for, he finds time hang heavy on his hands; he remains morally and spiritually asleep; and his position in society is often no higher than that of a polypus over which the tide floats.

> " His only labor is to kill the time,
> And labor dire it is, and weary woe."

Yet the rich man, inspired by a right spirit, will spurn idleness as unmanly; and if he bethink him of the responsibilities which attach to the possession of wealth and property, he will feel even a higher call to work than men of poorer lot. This, however, must be admitted to be by no means the practice of life. The golden mean of Agur's perfect prayer, is, perhaps, the best lot of all, if we did but know it : " Give me neither poverty nor riches; feed me with food convenient for me."—*Smiles.*

## FAILURE OF RICH MEN'S SONS.

THE president of one of our largest banks said, a short time ago, that a rich man's son had just left his place, and he was the last man of the kind he should ever employ. The man was faithful, honest, and fulfilled intelligently and well all the duties required of him; but just as he had become accustomed to his work, he found out that it was too confining, and a raw clerk had to be put in his place.

A bad look-out this for rich young men; but it is the old story repeated for the thousandth time. If rich men's sons will not endure the drudgery by which nearly all their fathers secured money and position, they must take a secondary place in the next generation; and oftener they drop out of sight amid the idle, worthless herd, if, indeed they escape an association with loafers and criminals.

Nearly every man in any leading position in the community began life poor. Let the sons of our rich men take warning and go to work honestly and faithfully every day, if they hope to fill the positions honorably held by their fathers.

---

## TRUE RESPECTABILITY.

RESPECTABILITY, in its best sense, is good. The respectable man is one worthy of regard, literally worth turning back to look at. But the respectability that consists in merely keeping up appearances is not worth looking at in any sense. Far better and more respectable is the good poor man than the bad rich one—better the humble silent man than the agreeable, well-appointed rogue, who keeps his carriage. A well-balanced and well-stored mind, a life full of useful purpose, whatever the position occupied in it may be—is of far greater importance than average worldly respectability. The highest object of life we take to be, to form a manly character, and to work out the best development possible, of body and spirit—of mind, conscience, heart and soul. This is the end; all else ought to be regarded but as the means. Accordingly, that is not the most successful life in which a man gets the most pleasure, the most money, the most power or place, honor or fame; but that in which a man gets the most manhood, and performs the greatest amount of useful work and of human duty. Money is power after its sort, it is true; but intelligence, public spirit, and moral virtue, are powers too, and far nobler ones. " Let others plead for pensions," wrote Lord Collingwood to a friend; " I can be rich without money, by endeavoring to be superior to everything poor. I would have my services to my country unstained by any interested motive; and old Scott* and I can go on in our cabbage-garden without much greater expense than formerly." On

* His old gardener. Collingwood's favorite amusement was gardening.

another occasion he said, " I have motives for my conduct which I would not give in exchange for a hundred pensions."

The making of a fortune may no doubt enable some people to " enter society," as it is called; but to be esteemed there, they must possess qualities of mind, manners, or heart, else they are merely rich people, nothing more.   There are men " in society " now, as rich as Crœsus, who have no consideration extended towards them, and elicit no respect.   For why?   They are but as money-bags, their only power is in their till.   The men of mark in society—the guides and rulers of opinion—the really successful and useful men—are not necessarily rich men; but men of sterling character, of disciplined experience, and of moral excellence.—*Smiles.*

## LIVING TOO HIGH.

MIDDLE-CLASS people are too apt to live up to their incomes, if not beyond them; affecting a degree of " style " which is most unhealthy in its effect upon society at large.   There is an ambition to bring up boys as gentlemen, or rather " genteel " men; though the result frequently is, only to make them gents.   They acquire a taste for dress, style, luxuries and amusements, which can never form any solid foundation for manly or gentlemanly character; and the result is, that we have a vast number of gingerbread young gentry thrown upon the world, who remind one of the abandoned hulls sometimes picked up at sea, with only a monkey on board.

We keep up appearances too often at the expense of honesty; and, though we may not be rich, yet we must seem to be so. We have not the courage to go patiently onward in the condition of life in which it has pleased God to call us; but must needs live in some fashionable state to which we ridiculously please to call ourselves. There is a constant struggle and pressure for front seats in the social amphitheatre; in the midst of which all noble self-denying resolve is trodden down, and many fine natures are inevitably crushed to death. What waste and misery this leads to we need not describe.—*Smiles.*

## APPLICATION AND PERSEVERANCE.

WITHOUT application and perseverance, if we rise at all, we shall—to use a common expression—" go up like a rocket and come down like a stick." Sydney Smith says: " The prevailing idea with young people, has been the incom-

4

patibility of labor and genius; and therefore, from the fear of being thought dull, they have thought it necessary to remain ignorant. It would go very far to destroy the absurd and pernicious association of genius and idleness, to show that the greatest poets, orators, statesmen, and historians—men of the most imposing and brilliant talents—have actually labored as hard as the makers of dictionaries and arrangers of indexes; and the most obvious reason why they have been superior to other men, is, that they have taken more pains than other men.

"Gibbon was in his study every morning, winter and summer, at six o'clock; Burke was the most laborious and indefatigable of human beings; Leibnitz was never out of his library; Pascal killed himself by study; Cicero narrowly escaped death from the same cause; Milton was at his books with as much regularity as a merchant or an attorney; he had mastered all the knowledge of his time; so had Homer; Raphael lived but thirty-seven years, and in that short space carried the art of painting so far beyond what it had before reached, that he appears to stand alone as a model to his successors."

Dalton, the chemist, always repudiated the notion of his being "a genius," attributing everything which he had accomplished to simple industry and accumulation.

Disraeli the elder, held that the secret of all success consisted in being master of your subject, such a result being only attainable through continuous application and study.

Newton, when asked by what means he had worked out his wonderful discoveries, modestly replied, " By always thinking unto them."

A great point is to get the working quality well trained. Facility comes with labor. Nothing can be accomplished without it. Continuous application will effect marvellous results in the commonest of things. It may seem a simple thing to play upon a violin ; yet what a long and laborious practice it requires! Giardini, when asked by a youth how long it would take to learn it, replied, " Twelve hours a day for twenty years together."

· When Taglioni, the great danseuse, was preparing herself for her evening performance, she would, after a severe two hours' lesson from her father, fall down exhausted, and had to be undressed, spunged, and resuscitated, totally unconscious. Success was attained only at a price like this. Less than half of such application devoted to self culture, could scarcely fail in insuring success. Progress, however, as a rule, is slow. Wonders cannot be achieved at once ; and we must be satisfied to advance in improvement as we walk step by step.  It has been said, that *"to know how to wait* is the great secret of success."  Sow first, then reap ; and oftentimes we must be content to look forward patiently in hope ; the fruit best worth waiting for often ripens the slowest.  " Time and patience," says the Eastern proverb, " change the  mulberry leaf to satin."

———

The greatest results in life are usually attained by simple means, and the exercise of ordinary qualities. The common life of every day, with its cares, necessities, and duties, affords ample opportunity for acquiring experience of the best kind ; and its most beaten paths provide the true worker with abundant scope for effort and room for self-improvement.  The great high-road of human welfare lies along the old highway of steadfast well-doing ; and they who are the most persistent, and work in the truest spirit, will invariably be the most successful.

Fortune has often been blamed for her blindness ; but fortune is not so blind as men are.  Those who look into practical life will find that fortune is usually on the side of the industrious, as the winds and waves are on the side of the best navigators.  Success treads on the heels of every right effort ; and though it is possible to overestimate success to the extent of almost deifying it, as is sometimes done, still, in any worthy pursuit, it is meritorious.   Nor are the qualities necessary to insure success at all extraordinary.   They may, for the most part, be summed up in these two—common sense and perseverance.—*Smiles.*

## *SEDULITY AND DILIGENCE.*

THERE is no such prevalent workman as sedulity and diligence.   A man would wonder at the mighty things which have been done by degrees and gentle augmentations.   Diligence and moderation are the best steps whereby to climb to any excellency.   Nay, it is rare if there be any other way. The heavens send not down their rain in floods, but by drops and dewy distillations.   A man is neither good, nor wise, nor rich, at once : yet softly creeping up these hills, he shall every day better his prospect ; till at last he gains the top.   Now he learns a virtue, and then he damns a vice.   An hour in a day may much profit a man in his study, when he makes it stint and custom.   Every year something laid up, may in time make a stock great.   Nay, if a man does but save, he shall increase ; and though when the grains are scattered, they be next to nothing, yet together

they will swell the heap.   He that has the patience to
attend small profits, may quickly grow to thrive and
purchase ; they be easier to accomplish, and come
thicker.   So, he that from everything collects somewhat, shall in time get a treasury of wisdom.   And
when all is done, for man, this is the best way.   It is
for God, and for Omnipotency, to do mighty things in
a moment ; but, *degreeingly* to grow to greatness, is the
course that he hath left for man.—*Feltham.*

## GOOD COUNSEL.

FURNISH *yourselves with a rich variety of ideas ;*
acquaint yourselves with things ancient and
modern ; things natural, civil, and religious ;
things domestic and national ; things of your native
land and of foreign countries ; things present, past,
and future ; and, above all, be well acquainted with
God and yourselves ; learn animal nature, and the
workings of your own spirits.

The way of attaining such an extensive treasure of
ideas is, with diligence to apply yourself to read the
best books ; converse with the most knowing and the
wisest of men, and endeavor to improve by every person in whose company you are ; suffer no hour to pass

away in a lazy idleness, in impertinent chattering, or useless trifles; visit other cities and countries when you have seen your own, under the care of one who can teach you to profit by traveling, and to make wise observations; indulge a just curiosity in seeing the wonders of art and nature; search into things yourselves, as well as learn them from others; be acquainted with men as well as books; learn all things as much as you can at first hand; and let as many of your ideas as possible be the representations of things, and not merely the representations of other men's ideas; thus your soul, like some noble building, shall be richly furnished with original paintings, and not with mere copies.

*Use the most proper methods to retain that treasure of ideas which you have acquired;* for the mind is ready to let many of them slip, unless some pains and labor be taken to fix them upon the memory.

And more especially let those ideas be laid up and preserved with the greatest care, which are most directly suited, either to your eternal welfare as a Christian, or to your particular station and profession in this life; for though the former rule recommends a universal acquaintance with things, yet it is but a more general and superficial knowledge that is required or expected of any man, in things which are utterly

foreign to his own business; but it is necessary you
should have a more particular and accurate acquaintance with those things that refer to your peculiar
province and duty in this life, or your happiness in
another.— *Watts.*

---

## COURAGE OF HOPE.

HOPE is like the sun, which, as we journey
towards it, casts the shadow of our burden behind us.  One of the most cheerful and
courageous, because one of the most hopeful of
workers, was Carey, the missionary.  When in India,
it was no uncommon thing for him to weary out three
pundits, who officiated as his clerks, in one day, he
himself taking rest only in change of employment.
Carey, himself the son of a shoemaker, was supported
in his labors by Ward, the son of a carpenter, and
Marshman, the son of a weaver.  By their labors, a
magnificent college was erected at Serampere; sixteen
flourishing stations were established; the Bible was
translated into sixteen languages, and the seeds were
sown of a beneficent moral revolution in British India.
Carey was never ashamed of the humbleness of his
origin.  On one occasion when at the Governor-
General's table, he overheard an officer opposite him

asking another loud enough to be heard, whether Carey had once been a shoemaker. " No, sir," exclaimed Carey immediately, " only a cobbler."

But to wait patiently, men must labor cheerfully. Cheerfulness and diligence are the life and soul of success, as well as happiness ; perhaps the very highest pleasure in life consisting in conscientious, brisk, hard working—energy, confidence, and every other good quality mainly depending upon it.

Laborers for the public good, especially, have to work long and patiently, often uncheered by the prospect of immediate recompense or result. The seeds they sow often lie hidden under the winter's snow, and before the spring comes, the husbandman may have gone to his rest.

## CHOOSE GOOD COMPANIONS.

TWO are better than one, and you will find it both protection and incentive if you can secure a faithful friend; and in some respects better than two are the many; therefore you cannot do more wisely than seek out in the Young Men's Society a wider companionship; and whilst instructed by the information of some, and strengthened by the firmer faith or larger experience of others, there are import

ant themes on which you will learn to think with pre-
cision, and in the exercise of public speaking you will
either acquire a useful talent or will turn it to good
account.—*Hamilton.*

———

## *LOVE OF KNOWLEDGE.*

SYDNEY SMITH, writing on this subject, uses
the following language : " I solemnly declare,
that but for the love of knowledge, I should
consider the life of the meanest hedger and ditcher as
preferable to that of the greatest and richest man in
existence ; for the fire of our minds is like the fires
which the Persians burn in the mountains, it flames
night and day, and is immortal, and not to be
quenched ! Upon something it must act and feed—
upon the pure spirit of knowledge, or upon the foul
dregs of polluting passions. Therefore, when I say,
in conducting your understanding, love knowledge
with a great love, with a vehement love, with a love
co-eval with life—what do I say but love innocence,
love virtue, love purity of conduct, love that which,
if you are rich and great, will vindicate the blind
fortune which has made you so, and make men call it
justice ; love that which, if you are poor, will render
your poverty respectable, and make the proudest feel

it unjust to laugh at the meanness of your fortunes ; love that which will comfort you, adorn you, and never quit you—which will open to you the kingdom of thought, and all the boundless regions of conception, as an asylum against the cruelty, the injustice, and the pain that may be your lot in the world—that which will make your motives habitually great and honorable, and light up in an instant a thousand noble disdains at the very thought of meanness and of fraud.

" Therefore, if any young man has embarked his life in pursuit of knowledge, let him go in without doubting or fearing the event, let him not be intimidated by the cheerless beginnings of knowledge, by the darkness from which she springs, by the difficulties which hover around her, by the wretched habitations in which she dwells, by the want and sorrow which sometimes journey in her train ; but let him ever follow her as the angel that guards him, and as the genius of his life, she will bring him out at last into the light of day, and exhibit him to the world comprehensive in acquirements, fertile in resources, rich in imagination, strong in reasoning, prudent and powerful above his fellows in all the relations and in all the offices of life."

Different people love different kinds of knowledge ;

but there are some who would like to excel in everything good.  The  mistake of many is in their trying
to acquire knowledge which they do not love—in let-
ting their ambition to excel overmaster them—and the
result is that there are large numbers of half educated
people in the world  who  are  like  the  child  and  the
apples.  A gentleman  bought  a  lot  of apples, and
offered one to a little child.  It was pleased, and took
it eagerly.  He  then  offered it another, which it also
grasped.  He  kept  giving  it  the  apples  one  after
another, the  child reaching for them just as fast as he
offered them, until at last its little arms were  full, and
in reaching for the last one, all  the  others  rolled  on
the ground.  Then  it cried.  It  had  tried  to  grasp
more than it could hold.

---

## SELF-DENIAL.

THE lesson of self-denial is far beyond any other
in importance.  It must be repeated a thousand times over before it is really learnt by
heart, but oh, how worthy the pains!  Happy is he
who has learnt not to seek for what is pleasant, not to
shrink from what is painful, but to go on doing everything that he knows to be good, and kind, and right,

ın utter disregard of self.   How a man might ennoble
and invigorate his life if he would work this principle
into the very grain of his mind, and strenuously act
upon it, invariably striving not after what would be
pleasantest ; but what would be best.   In fact, it is the
very essence of all that is good and great in human
life ; and not only so, but it is the true road to happiness.   This is doubtless what our Saviour means when
he says that he that hath left home and brethren for
his sake shall receive an hundred fold even in his life.
—*Charles Buxton.*

## *IDLENESS NOT HAPPINESS.*

THE most common error of men and women is
that of looking for happiness somewhere outside of useful work.   It has never yet been
found when thus sought, and never will be while the
world stands ; and the sooner this truth is learned the
better for everyone.   If you doubt the proposition,
glance around among your friends and aequaintances,
and select those who appear to have the most enjoyment in life.   Are they the idlers and pleasure-seekers,
or the earnest workers ?   We know what your answer
will be.   Of all the miserable human beings it has
been our fortune or misfortune to know. they were the

most wretched who had retired from useful employment to enjoy themselves; while the slave at his
enforced labor, or the hungry toiler for bread, were
supremely happy in comparison.

———

## PROCRASTINATION.

MRS. WHITNEY says, in one of her books,
that " the things which are crowded out of a
life are the test of that life," and we believe
that the saying is true in its widest sense.   Examine
our lives closely, and we shall find that we constantly
delude ourselves with the idea that we would accomplish certain things if we had time, when, in truth,
we have no real desire for those things.   One person
will say that *reading* is out of the question; another
will bewail the impossibility of maintaining social
relations; a third will avow that charitable or benevo-
lent enterprises would delight her if she might engage
in them; and all the time these good people are com-
forting themselves with a fallacy.   The things for which
they *do* find time are the things they prefer.   The
things which are crowded out are the things they
would not choose if life lay unemployed before them.
   Scores of wives and mothers are busied constantly

with their family cares, but not one in every score loves music enough to steal time for practice. Hundreds of young men are forced by stress of circumstances to work hard for daily subsistence, but only one in a thousand, perhaps, conquers the difficulty of his position, and makes a name for himself. This one might not have found his way easier or its upward steps less tiresome, but he wanted to succeed, and so wanting, let nothing needful be crowded out.

---

## VALUE OF TIME.

JOHN LOCKE, the English philosopher, was a favorite with many of the great noblemen of his age. They liked his robust sense and ready wit, and enjoyed even the sharp reproofs in which he occasionally indulged. On one occasion he had been invited to meet a select party at Lord Ashley's. When he came they were playing at cards, and continued absorbed in the game for two or three hours.

For some time Locke looked on, and then began to write diligently in a blank book taken from his pocket. At length they asked him what he was writing. He answered:

" My lords, I am improving myself the best I can

in your company; for, having impatiently waited this honor of being present at such a meeting of the wise men and great wits of the age, I thought I could not do better than write down your conversation, and here I have in substance all that has passed for this hour or two."

The noble lords were so ashamed at the written record of their frivolous talk, that they at once stopped card-playing, and began the discussion of an important subject.

———

Thomas Carlyle has uttered even a more pungent reproof of idle talk: " If we can permit God Almighty," he says, " to write down our conversation, thinking it good enough for him, any poor Boswell need not scruple to work his will."

———

## VALUE OF ODD MOMENTS.

ELIHU BURRITT, the learned blacksmith, says: " All that I have accomplished, or expect, or hope to accomplish, has been and will be by that plodding, patient, persevering process of accretion which builds the ant-heap, particle by particle, thought by thought, fact by fact. If I was ever actuated by ambition, its highest and warmest aspiration reached no further than the hope to set before the young men of my country an example in employing those invaluable fragments of time called odd moments ! "

---

## BEHIND TIME.

A RAILROAD TRAIN was rushing along at almost lightning speed. A curve was just ahead, beyond which was a station at which the cars usually passed each other. The conductor was late, so late that the period during which the down train was to wait had nearly elapsed, but he hoped yet to pass the curve safely. Suddenly a locomotive dashed into sight right ahead. In an instant there was a collision. A shriek, a shock, and fifty souls were in eternity; and all because a conductor had been *behind time.*

A great battle was going on. Column after column had been precipitated for eight mortal hours on the enemy posted along the ridge of a hill. The summer sun was sinking to the west, reinforcements for the obstinate defenders were already in sight; it was necessary to carry the position with one final charge, or everything would be lost

5

A powerful corps had been summoned from across the country, and if it came up in season, all would yet be well. The great conqueror, confident in its arrival, formed his reserve into an attacking column, and ordered them to charge the enemy. The whole world knows the result. Grouchy* failed to appear; the imperial guard was beaten back; Waterloo was lost. Napoleon died a prisoner at St. Helena, because one of his marshals was *behind time.*

A leading firm in commercial circles had long struggled against bankruptcy. As it had enormous assets in California, it expected remittances by a certain day, and if the sums promised arrived, its credit, its honor, and its future prosperity would be preserved. But week after week elapsed without bringing the gold. At last came the fatal day on which the firm had bills maturing to enormous amounts. The steamer was telegraphed at daybreak ; but it was found, on inquiry, that she brought no funds, and the house failed. The next arrival brought nearly half a million to the insolvents, but it was too late; they were ruined because their agent, in remitting, had been *behind time.*

---

* Napoleon Bonaparte, Emperor of France, was defeated by the allies under the Duke of Wellington, at Waterloo, June 18, 1815. Marshal Grouchy was expected to aid the Emperor with a body of troops, but failed to appear.

A condemned man was led out for execution. He had taken human life, but under circumstances of the greatest provocation, and public sympathy was active in his behalf. Thousands had signed the petition for a reprieve; a favorable answer had been expected the night before, and though it had not come, even the sheriff felt confident that it would yet arrive in season. Thus the morning passed without the appearance of the messenger. The last moment was up. The prisoner took his place in the drop, the cap was drawn over his eyes, the bolt was drawn, and a lifeless body swung revolving in the wind. Just at that moment a horseman came into sight, galloping down hill, his steed covered with foam. He carried a packet in his right hand, which he waved rapidly to the crowd. He was the express rider with the reprieve. But he had come too late. A comparatively innocent man had died an ignominious death because a watch had been five minutes too slow, making its bearer arrive *behind time.*

It is continually so in life. The best laid plans, the most important affairs, the fortunes of individuals, the weal of nations, honor, happiness, life itself, are daily sacrificed because somebody is " behind time." There are others who put off reformation year by year, till death seizes them, and they perish unrepentant, because forever "behind time." Five minutes in a crisis is worth years. It is but a little period, yet it has often saved a fortune or redeemed a people. If there is one virtue that should be cultivated more than another by him who would succeed in life, it is punctuality; if there is one error that should be avoided, it is being *behind time.—Freeman Hunt.*

## ONE BY ONE.

One by one the sands are flowing,
  One by one the moments fall;
Some are coming, some are going;
  Do not strive to catch them all.

One by one thy duties wait thee;
  Let thy whole strength go to each;
Let no future dreams elate thee;
  Learn thou first what these can teach

One by one (bright gifts from heaven)
  Joys are sent thee here below;
Take them readily when given—
  Ready, too, to let them go.

One by one thy griefs shall meet thee;
  Do not fear an armed band;
One will fade as others greet thee—
  Shadows passing through the land.

Do not laugh at life's long sorrow;
  See how small each moment's pain:
God will help thee for to-morrow;
  Every day begin again.

Every hour, that fleets so slowly,
  Has its task to do or bear;
Luminous the crown, and holy,
  If thou set each gem with care.

Hours are golden links—God's token
  Reaching heaven; but one by one,
Take them, lest the chain be broken
  Ere thy pilgrimage be done.

—MISS PROCTOR.

## LEARNING IN YOUTH.

DANIEL WEBSTER once told a good story in a speech, and was asked where he got it. "I have had it laid up in my head for fourteen years, and never had a chance to use it until to-day," said he.

My little friend wants to know what good it will do to learn the "rule of three," or to commit a verse of the Bible. The answer is this: "Sometime you will need that very thing. Perhaps it may be twenty years before you can make it fit in just the right place; but it will be just in place sometime.   Then, if you don't have it, you will be like the hunter who had no ball in his rifle when a bear met him.

"Twenty-five years ago my teacher made me study surveying," said a man who had lately lost his property, "and now I am glad of it.   It is just in place. I can get a good situation and high salary."

---

## THE POWER OF KINDNESS.

**D**URING the days of the French convention, Penel, the master of the lunatic asylum, desired permission to employ a new method for the recovery of its inmates.   It was usual then to treat these helpless creatures as brutes; to scourge them with stripes, to load them with chains, and fasten them securely to the floors of their cells.   Hundreds were thus bound when Penel bethought him of a more excellent way.   He proposed to the convention a radical change of treatment; especially he recommended that the insane be treated as patients, and be freed from their chains.   While the convention yielded its consent, the president, M. Caithon, regarded the keeper as crazy.   The day came for the experiment to be made, and the keeper released, first of all, a wretched man who had been bound for forty years. This victim of ignorant cruelty did not destroy his benefactor, as Caithon had expected, but quietly staggered to the window of his cell, and, looking out through the tears that filled his eyes, on the placid sky, gently murmured, " Beautiful, oh ! how beautiful ! "

Shall human kindness have such power to subdue and to rekindle the dying flame of reason, and heavenly grace be impotent to soften the hard heart and to beget the life of righteousness? No. I am persuaded when grace enters the dark prison-house of sin, and is permitted to break the fetters of iniquity, the freed soul, amazed at the matchless clemency, will not merely cry " Beautiful, beautiful," but, by the " beauty of holiness " clothing thought and deed, will show forth its increasing gratitude, love and praise.—*Rev. George C. Lorimer, D. D.*

---

## LET BYGONES BE BYGONES.

LET bygones be bygones; if bygones were clouded
By aught that occasioned a pang of regret,
O, let them in darkest oblivion be shrouded:
'Tis wise and 'tis kind to forgive and forget.

Let bygones be bygones, and good be extracted
From ill, over which it is folly to fret;

The wisest of mortals have foolishly acted—
. The kindest are those who forgive and forget.

Let bygones be bygones; O cherish no longer
  The thought that the sun of affection has set;
Eclipsed for a moment, its rays will be stronger
  If you, like a Christian, forgive and forget.

Let bygones be bygones, your heart will be lighter
  When kindness of yours with reception has met;
The flame of your heart will be purer and brighter
  If, God-like, you strive to forgive and forget.

Let bygones be bygones; O, purge out the leaven
  Of malice, and try an example to set
To others, who, craving the mercy of heaven,
  Are sadly too slow to forgive and forget.

Let bygones be bygones; remember how deeply
  To heaven's forbearance we all are in debt!
They value God's infinite goodness too cheaply
  To heed not the precept, "Forgive and Forget."

                  —CHAMBER'S JOURNAL.

## THOUGHTLESSNESS OF YOUTH.

IN general, I have no patience with people who talk about the "thoughtlessness of youth," indulgently. I had infinitely rather hear of thoughtless old age, and the indulgence due to *that*.

When a man has done his work, and nothing can in any way be materially altered in his fate, let him forget his toil and jest with his fate, if he will; but what excuse can you find for willfulness of thought, at the very time when every crisis of future fortune hangs on your decisions?    A youth thoughtless! when all the happiness of his home forever depends on the chances. or the passions of an hour!    A youth thoughtless! when his every act is a foundation stone of future conduct, and every imagination a fountain of life or death!    Be thoughtless in any after years, rather than now—though indeed there is only one place where a man may be nobly thoughtless—his death-bed.    No thinking should ever be left to be done there.—*Ruskin.*

---

## WASHINGTON ON SWEARING.

ON the 29th of July, 1779, one hundred years ago, General Washington issued a special order, at West Point, in reference to the practice of profanity:

"Many and pointed orders have been issued against that unmeaning and abominable custom of swearing, notwithstanding which, with much regret, the General observes that it prevails, if possible, more than ever;

his feelings are continually wounded by the oaths and imprecations of the soldiers whenever he is in hearing of them.

"The name of that Being from whose bountiful goodness we are permitted to exist and enjoy the comforts of life, is incessantly imprecated and profaned in a manner as wanton as it is shocking. For the sake, therefore, of religion, decency and order, the General hopes and trusts that officers of every rank will use their influence and authority to check a vice which is as unprofitable as wicked and shameful.

"If officers would make it an unavoidable rule to reprimand, and, if that does not do, punish soldiers for offences of this kind, it could not fail of having the desired effect."

————

## BEWARE OF LITTLE SINS.

IT is a solemn thought this of the steady continuous aggravation of sin in the individual character. Surely nothing can be small which goes to make up that rapidly growing total. Beware of the little beginnings which "eat as doth a canker." Beware of the slightest deflection from the straight line of right. If there be two lines, one straight and the other going off at the sharpest angle, you have only to produce both far enough, and there will be room between them for all the space that separates hell from heaven! Beware of lading your souls with the weight of small single sins. We heap upon ourselves by slow, steady accretion through a lifetime the weight, that though it is gathered by grains, crushes the soul. There is nothing heavier than sand. You may lift it by particles. It drifts in atoms, but heaped upon a man it will break his bones, and blown over the land it buries pyramid and sphinx, the temples of gods and the homes of men beneath its barren, solid waves. The leprosy gnaws the flesh off a man's bones, and joints and limbs drop off—he is a living death. So with every soul that is under the dominion of these lying desires—it is slowly rotting away piecemeal, " waxing corrupt according to the lusts of deceit."

---

## CONSCIENTIOUSNESS IN SMALL THINGS.

A WOMAN employed a man to paint a house she had just built. The painter was a member of a Christian church, active in the prayer-meeting and in church work, and apparently a man of exemplary piety. His work was seemingly well done, but it was afterwards discovered that he had slighted his work in places where he thought the neglect would not be noticed. His employer remarked: "I have discounted that man's piety and prayers ever since. I prefer Christians who will fill up the nail holes with putty, and paint the tops of the doors in the upper story." "It has often seemed to us," says the *Examiner*, "that this man was not an exceptional case. How many professed Christians fail to realize that piety has a connection with paint and putty—that the little things of life are the truest, as they are the severest tests of Christian character. Anyone who has to employ others to do work for him knows how rare it is to find a man or woman who is conscientious about small things; who never 'scamps' his work, and never wastes his employer's time or stock." The *Examiner* adds:

"The cultivation of a greater conscientiousness with regard to the little things of everyday life, which are commonly considered to have no bearing on piety, is one of the almost universal needs, even among Christian people. The painter Opie replied to a query as to how he mixed his colors, 'With brains, sir.' The best type of Christian character must be that of the man who mixes his daily work with conscience, and strives to do everything, even the most insignificant, as unto the Lord. Until this shall be the standard of everyday Christian living, there must be a great deal done in the way of discounting piety and prayers."—*Christian Union.*

---

## EFFECTS OF WORRY.

WORRYING is one of the great drawbacks to happiness. Most of it can be avoided if we only determine not to let trifles annoy us; for the largest amount of worrying is caused by the smallest trifles.

A writer in *Chambers' Journal* says : "That the effects of worry are more to be dreaded than those of simple hard work, is evident from noting the class of persons who suffer most from the effects of overstrain. The case-book of the physician shows that it is the speculator, the betting man, the railway manager, the great merchant, the superintendent of large manufacturing or commercial works, who most frequently exhibit the symptoms of cerebral exhaustion. Mental cases accompanied by suppressed emotion, occupations liable to great vicissitudes of fortune, and those which involve the bearing on the mind of a multiplicity of intricate details, eventually break down the lives of the strongest.   In estimating what may be called the staying powers of different minds under hard work, it is always necessary to take early training into account. A young man, cast suddenly into a position involving great care and responsibility, will break down; whereas, had he been gradually habituated to this position, he would have performed its duties without difficulty.   It is probably for this reason that the professional classes generally suffer less from the effects of overstrain than others.   They have had a long course of preliminary training, and their work comes on them by degrees ; therefore, when it does come in excessive quantity, it finds them prepared for it.   Those, on the other hand, who suddenly vault into a position requiring severe mental toil, generally die before their time."

## KEEP YOUR TEMPER.

YOU will accomplish nothing by losing it.   Many men date their failure in business to some hasty and ill-considered statement made during a fit of temper.   When things go awry, business is dull, and the prospect is dark ahead, it is very poor consolation to indulge in passionate and angry remarks to those with whom you are associated.   The frown on a man's face is a good indication of the state of the feelings within. The world judges men by their outward conduct and behavior, and ill-natured, cross-grained men rarely become successful.

Solomon says : " He that is slow to anger is better than the mighty ; and he that ruleth his spirit than he that taketh a city ; " " Seest thou a man that is hasty in his words ? there is more hope of a fool than of him." Difficulties disappear when met calmly and resolutely ; they increase with ill-nature and anger. Keep your temper.

---

## TRUTH AND FALSEHOOD.

THE abuse which you pour forth on me will throw no light on our controversy, and the menaces with which you assail me will not hinder me from defending myself. You think that you have force and impunity on your side; but on mine I think that I have truth and innocence. A strange and long warfare it is, when violence endeavors to oppress truth. All the efforts of violence can avail nothing to weaken truth, and serve only to make it supreme. All the light of truth can avail nothing to arrest violence, and only provokes it the more. When force combats force, the stronger destroys the weaker;

when arguments are opposed to arguments, the truer
and more convincing confound and scatter those
which rest only on vanity and falsehood; but violence
and truth are powerless against each other. Yet think
not that they are therefore on a level. Between them
is this absolute difference, that the course of violence
is limited by the decree of God, who compels it to
promote the glory of the truth which it attacks; while
truth subsists eternally, and finally triumphs over its
enemies, because it is eternal and strong even as God
himself.—*Pascal.*

————

Truth is the most powerful thing in the world, since
fiction can only please us by its resemblance to it.—
*Shaftesbury.*

————

Truth is its own evidence, as the lightning flash is,
as the blessed sunshine is.—*F. W. Robertson.*

————

## CHARACTERS.

OOKING over all the varieties of character with
a view to classification, we find that some are
the result mainly of conditions that are physical. Mere temperament often determines the whole
complexion of a life, explaining the characteristic dif-

ferences between some men and others. One man, owing purely to physical conditions, is morbid and melancholy. He sees everything under a cloud. He looks naturally at the dark side of things. If you take him to the bright side, he brings a shadow with him and makes this side as gloomy as the other. Another man, blessed with a sanguine temperament, has a fountain of cheerfulness and hope within him. He looks naturally at the bright side; brightens even the dark side, when he comes round to it, by his own sunshine. Whatever is naturally pleasant he rejoices in. He is a child of the light. Even if a disaster occur, he is glad that it is no worse. The Dutchman who fell from the ladder and broke his leg, and expressed to his distracted family his delight that it was not his neck, must have been a man of this type. Mr. Sanguine to every cloud sees a silver lining. If you consult him in misfortune, he says: " You will soon get over it. I'll tell you what to do."

The gloomy man, on the other hand, says: "I told you it would come to this," and shakes his head portentously, as if he were satisfied that this is only the beginning of your troubles. To Mr. Croaker even pleasure is poisoned by the thought of how soon it may be taken away. If he finds you particularly jovial, it reminds him of a former occasion, on which

6

just such merriment was interrupted by some fearful intelligence. He hopes, with a portentous look, that it may not be so this time again.

Mr. Croaker is peculiarly appropriate at a funeral; but woe betide the picnic or wedding party to which, in a moment of infatuation, he has been invited. The only hope lies in Mr. Sanguine being there also. Mr. Sanguine is always a refuge and wall of defense, whom you should take care to have with you in embarrassing circumstances or when called on to pass through some ordeal like that of having to inspect and give your verdict upon your friend's first baby. If you are sensitive, like some folk, you will find that a stiff trial. You go to the inspection aware, of course, that both father and mother regard this baby as one of the finest that has ever been born, and that they have been fortified in this conviction by the doctor. Now, if it should tnrn out to be an ugly little imp, what are you to say? How are you to look? Have Mr. Sanguine with you? Mr. Sanguine will see something to admire in any baby that ever was born. If it is one of those lively infants that seem all on springs, Mr. Sanguine will cry: " What a fine fellow ! What life ! What energy ! " If it be one of those dull, torpid lumps of humanity that glare straight forward with a fishy glare, gorgonizing you from head to foot, Mr. Sanguine will exclaim,

"What a thoughtful child! What steadiness! What brain!" If the child had been born with a leg on the top of its head, Mr. Sanguine would instantly have been struck with the advantage this would give it, in the event of it tumbling wrong end down.—*Rev. Davia Macrae.*

———

Character has many ways of manifesting itself; and those may be in the right who regard a man's chirography as one of these. Shelley, in one of his letters, passes judgment upon two of his brother poets, with this sort of testimony in view, as follows: "The hand-writing of Ariosto is a small, firm, and pointed character, expressing, as I should say, a strong and keen, but circumscribed energy of mind; that of Tasso is large, free and flowing, except that there is a checked expression in the midst of its flow, which brings the letters into a smaller compass than one expected from the beginning of the word. It is the symbol of an intense and earnest mind, exceeding at times its own depths, and admonished to return by the chilliness of the waters of oblivion striking upon its adventurous feet." It may be well for us all to remember that there are more open doors than we may imagine, through which scrutinizing eyes look in upon the secret places of our character.

Men seek retreats for themselves—houses in the country, sea-shores, and mountains; and thou, too, art wont to desire such things very much. But this is altogether a work of the most common men; for it is in thy power, whenever thou shalt choose, to retire into thyself. For nowhere, either with more quiet or more freedom from trouble, does a man retire than into his own soul, particularly when he has within him such thoughts, that by looking into them he is immediately in perfect tranquility. And I affirm that tranquility is nothing else than the good ordering of the mind.— *" Thoughts " of the Emperor Marcus Aurelius.*

---

We are all sculptors and painters, and our material is our own flesh, and blood, and bones. Any nobleness begins at once to refine a man's features; any meanness or sensuality, to imbrute them.—*Thoreau.*

---

As a storm following storm, and wave succeeding wave, give additional hardness to the shell that incloses the pearl, so do the storms and waves of life add force to the character of man.

---

Feelings come and go like light troops following the victory of the present; but principles, like troops of the line, are undisturbed and stand fast.—*Richter*

What a grand power is the power of thought! And what a grand being is man when he uses it aright; because, after all, it is the use made of it that is the important thing. Character comes out of thought; or rather thought comes out of character. The particular thoughts are like the blossoms on the trees; they tell of what kind it is. "As a man thinketh in his heart, so he is."—*Sir W. Raleigh.*

----

A soul immortal, spending all her fires,
Wasting her strength in strenuous idleness,
Thrown into tumult, raptured, or alarmed,
At aught this scene can threaten or indulge
Resembles ocean into tempest wrought
To waft a feather, or to drown a fly.      —YOUNG.

----

The heart will commonly govern the head; and it is certain that any strong passion, set the wrong way, will soon infatuate even the wisest of men; therefore the first part of wisdom is to watch the affections.—*Dr. Waterland.*

----

Modesty is to worth what shadows are in a painting; she gives to it strength and relief.—*La Bruuere.*

----

Actions, looks, words, steps, form the alphabet by which you may spell character.

Every man stamps his value on himself. The price we challenge for ourselves is given us. There does not live on earth a man, be his station what it may, that I despise myself. Man is made great or little by his own will.—*Schiller.*

———

No man has come to true greatness who has not felt in some degree that his life belongs to his race, and what God gives him he gives him for mankind.— *Phillips Brooks.*

———

Character is like bells which ring out sweet music, and which, when touched accidentally even, resound sweetly.

———

Men seldom improve when they have no other models than themselves to copy after.—*Goldsmith.*

———

You can not dream yourself into a character; you must hammer and forge yourself one.—*Froude.*

———

Never does a man portray his own character more vividly than in his manner of portraying another's.

———

The key to every man is his thought. Casual thoughts are sometimes of great value.

People that have their eyes opened will, at the very least, get their clothes washed. A neat, decent dress is often an early sign that a man is becoming careful who has hitherto been reckless; and new talk, new tempers, new estimates of things, are garments of the spiritual man, that show he has become a *new man*.

———

Christianity means to the merchant that he should be honest; to the judge it means that he should be just; to the servant, that he should be faithful; to the school-boy, that he should be diligent; to the street-sweeper, that he should sweep clean; to every worker, that his work shall be well done.

———

Conscience is the voice of the soul; the passions are the voice of the body.—*J. J. Rousseau.*

———

Manner is one of the greatest engines of influence ever given to man.—*Sunday Afternoon.*

———

Flattery is a false coin which has circulation only through our vanity.—*La Rochefoucauld.*

———

How can we expect a harvest of thought who have not had a seed-time of character?

No trait of character is rarer, none more admirable, than thoughtful independence of the opinions of others combined with a sensitive regard to the feelings of others.

———

## WISDOM AND GOODNESS.

I WOULD be good, I would be wise,
    For all men should. The wise man saith,
    "Folly is sin, and sin is death."
        But Fate denies
    What I demand for boons like these,
    If not a life, yet days of ease.

Not in this world of noise and care
    Is Wisdom won, however wooed;
    She must be sought in solitude,
        With thought and prayer!
She will not hear my hasty cries;
I have no leisure to be wise!

Who can be wise that can not fly
    These empty babblers, loud and vain;
    To whom there is no God but Gain?
        Alas! not I.
But this dark thought will still intrude,
There needs no leisure to be good!

———

Goodness is the only happiness.—*Socrates.*

If we can by honest effort change a wayworn thought to a manly purpose, encourage the halting mind to correct views, remove all prejudices, enkindle chaste desires, and strengthen a noble purpose, our efforts in life shall not be in vain. Feeble our efforts may be, as the breeze that kisses the mountain summit, yet it may be the morning breath that shall help on his mission of mercy, virtue and usefulness, some waiting pilgrim.

———

Whoever sincerely endeavors to do all the good he can will probably do much more than he imagines, or will ever know to the day of judgment, when the secrets of all hearts shall be manifest.

———

Better a cheap coffin and a plain funeral, after a useful, unselfish life, than a grand procession and a marble mausoleum, after a loveless, selfish life.

———

To do good to men is the great work of life; to make them true Christians is the greatest good we can do them.—*Dr. J. W. Alexander.*

———

If a man have love in his heart, he may talk in broken language, but it will be eloquence to those who listen.

The best recipe for going through life in an exquisite way with beautiful manner, is to feel that everybody, no matter how rich or how poor, need all the kindness they can get from others in the world.

———

There is as much greatness of mind in the owing of a good turn as in the doing of it, and we must no more force a requital out of season, than to be wanting in it.—*Seneca.*

———

Liberality, courtesy, benevolence, unselfishness, under all circumstances and toward all men—these qualities are to the world what the linchpin is to the rolling chariot.

———

To return good for good, is civil courtesy; evil for evil, malicious policy; evil for good, hateful ingratitude; good for evil, true Christian charity.—*Schlatter.*

———

Good men have the fewest fears. He has but one who fears to do wrong. He has a thousand who has overcome that one.

———

The wisely good man seeks to connect others with him, by the influence of that which separates him from them.

A cunning man is never a firm man, but an honest man is; a double-minded man is always unstable, a man of faith is firm as a rock; honesty is faith applied to worldly things, and faith is honesty quickened by the Spirit to the use of heavenly things.—*Edward Irving.*

———

To fill the sphere which Providence appoints is true wisdom; to discharge trusts faithfully and live exalted ideas, that is the mission of good men.

———

## ENERGY AND COURAGE.

ENERGY enables a man to force his way through irksome drudgery and dry details, and carries him onward and upward in every station in life. It accomplishes more than genius. Energy of will may be defined to be the very central power of character in a man—in a word, it is the Man himself. True hope is based on it—and it is hope that gives the real perfume to life. No blessing is equal to the possession of a stout heart. Charles IX., of Sweden, was a firm believer in the power of will, even in a youth. Laying his hand on the head of his youngest son, when engaged upon a difficult task, he exclaimed,

" He shall do it! he shall do it! " Nothing that is of real worth can be achieved without courageous work-ing. The timid and hesitating find everything impos-sible, chiefly because it seems so. The Scriptural injunction, " Whatsoever thy hand findeth to do, do it with all thy might," must be realized if you wish to succeed. It is pluck, tenacity, and determined perse-verance which wins soldiers' battles, and, indeed, every battle. It is the one neck nearer that wins the race and shows the blood; it is the one march more that wins the campaign; the five minutes' more persistent courage that wins the fight. Though your force be less than another's, you equal and out-master your opponent if you continue it longer and concentrate it more. The reply of the Spartan father, who said to his son, when complaining that his sword was too short, " Add a step to it," is applicable to everything in life.—*Smiles*.

## FORCE OF PURPOSE.

IT is *will*—force of purpose—that enables a man to do or be whatever he sets his mind on being or doing. No one ardently wishes to be sub-missive, patient, modest, or liberal, who does not become what he wishes.

"You are now at the age," said Lammenais once, addressing a gay youth, "at which a decision must be formed by you; a little later, and you may have to groan within the tomb which yourself have dug, without the power of rolling away the stone. That which the easiest becomes a habit in us is the will. Learn then to will strongly and decisively; thus fix your floating life, and leave it no longer to be carried hither and thither, like a withered leaf, by every wind that blows."

Buxton held the conviction that a young man might be very much what he pleased, provided he formed a strong resolution and held to it. Writing to one of his own sons, he once said, "You are now at that period of life in which you must make a turn to the right or the left. You must now give proofs of principle, determination, and strength of mind; or you must sink into idleness, and acquire the habits and character of a desultory, ineffective young man; and if once you fall to that point, you will find it no easy matter to rise again. I am sure that a young man may be very much what he pleases. In my own case it was so. * * * * Much of my happiness, and all my prosperity in life, have resulted from the change I made at your age. If you seriously resolve to be energetic and industrious, depend upon it that you will for your whole life have reason to rejoice that you were wise enough to form and to act upon that determination." As will, considered without regard to direction, is simply constancy, firmness, perseverance, it will be obvious that everything depends upon right direction and motives. Directed towards the enjoyment of the senses, the strong will may be a demon, and the intellect merely its debased slave; but directed towards good, the strong will is a king, and the intellect is then the minister of man's highest well-being.

"Where there is a will there is a way," is an old and true saying. He who resolves upon doing a thing, by that very resolution often scales the barriers to it, and secures its achievement.

To think we are able, is almost to be so—to determine upon attainment, is frequently attainment itself. Thus, earnest resolution has often seemed to have about it almost a savor of omnipotence. The strength of Suwarrow's character lay in his power of willing, and, like most resolute persons, he preached it up as a system. "You can only half will," he would say to people who failed. Like Richelieu and Napoleon, he would have the word "impossible" banished from the dictionary. "I don't know," "I can't," and "impossible," were words which he detested above all others. "Learn! Do! Try!" he would exclaim. His

biographer has said of him, that he furnished a remarkable illustration of what may be effected by the
energetic development and exercise of faculties, the
germs of which at least are in every human heart.

## PROMPTITUDE AND DECISION.

ENERGY usually displays itself in promptitude
and decision. When Ledyard, the traveler,
was asked by the African Association when he
would be ready to set out for Africa, he promptly answered, "To-morrow morning." Blucher's promptitude obtained for him the cognomen of "Marshal
Forwards" throughout the Prussian army. When
John Jervis, afterwards Earl St. Vincent, was asked
when he would be ready to join his ship, he replied,
"Directly." And when Sir Colin Campbell, appointed
to the command of the Indian army, was asked when
he could set out, his answer was, "To-morrow"—an
earnest of his subsequent success. For it is rapid decision, and a similar promptitude in action, such as
taking instant advantage of an enemy's mistakes, that
so often wins battles. "Every moment lost," said
Napoleon, "gives an opportunity for misfortune;"
and he used to say that he beat the Austrians because

they never knew the value of time; while they dawdled, he overthrew them. In many positions in life, "he who hesitates is lost." Endeavor, therefore, to be prompt and decisive in answer and action. Lack of decision has been the ruin of thousands of business men; while they considered, others acted, and so secured the advantage.

———

Decision of character is the one bright, golden apple, which every young man should strive in the beginning to pluck from the tree of life.—*Foster*.

———

Deeds always overbalance, and downright practice speaks more plainly than the fairest profession.

———

## *RICHES AND REFINEMENT.*

IT is a great mistake to confound riches and refinement, just as it is a great mistake to fancy that because a man is poor, he must be coarse and vulgar. Lord Jefferies, though seated in the highest tribunal in the realm, while pouring forth his brutal ribaldry, was a vulgar man; and a very vulgar man was Chancellor Thurlow, spouting oaths and obscenity at the table of the Prince of Wales. Bu' there was no vulgarity about James Ferguson, though herding sheep, while his eye watched Arcturus and the Pleiades, and his wistful spirit wandered through immensity; and, though seated at a stocking loom, there was no vulgarity in the youth who penned "The Star of Bethlehem;" the weaver boy, Henry Kirkewhite, was not a vulgar lad.—*James Hamilton.*

----

## THE STRENGTH OF SILENCE.

THERE is a mighty power in silence, and silence is frequently an evidence of power. There are many men so weak that they can not hold their tongues, or keep their mouths shut. The man who offends not in word is a perfect man, able to bridle the whole body. He who can control his tongue, can control his entire nature. Hence silence is a token of power, of reserved force. He who knows how to keep silence knows how to speak; and often his silence is more impressive than his speech. "Brilliant flashes of silence" is by no means a senseless expression. How often have we seen the babble of the foolish hushed by the silent glance of an earnest soul; how often the ribald jest or scurrilous word has died upon the lips when an indignant silence was the only reply

7

it could evoke. That man or that woman who can stand silent amid reproaches and accusations and sneers and scoffs, shows a degree of strength and power which falls not to the lot of every one.

———

The silent accomplish more than the noisy. The tail of the rattlesnake makes all the noise, but the head does all the execution.

———

## CORRECT SPEECH.

NOTHING bespeaks a true lady and gentleman or well-bred child more than the use of correct language, pure, clean speech. Cultivate my young friends, good English in every-day conversation. Unclean speech is in keeping with a smutty face, begrimed hands, and soiled clothes. Strange, how easy and almost unconsciously one slides into a careless slipshod way of talking, even when the rules of grammar are quite familiar. It is not uncommon to find people learned in all the rules of syntax who apply them to the art of writing, yet habitually talk incorrectly.

Early culture and association with refined persons are quite essential to give purity to speech ; but if one bas been unfortunately deprived of these, he should continually watch his words till he gets in the habit of using decent English, for nothing so unmistakably marks one with vulgarity, no matter how elegant is the outside covering, as shabby, low-born speech.

---

## COARSENESS.

ANY lack of refinement in one's manner, or any incivility in one's ordinary personal address, ought certainly to be a matter of regret to the person whose daily life displays such a defect.   But it is by no means uncommon for men and women to think, or to pretend they think, that rudeness of manner and neglect of the courtesies of life are evidences of a strong character; and that a coarse and uncivil habit of speech is an admirable proof that the speaker is a "plain, blunt man," who is above shams and pretences.

Now, while coarseness may exist along with strength of character and righteousness of life, it is always a blemish to them, and never a help.

Every one who is trying to lead a good life, should also try to lead a winsome and courteous life.   By abandoning gentleness of disposition and graciousness of word and deed, he throws away a means of growth and an effective weapon. It is almost always a grave mistake, in a matter of manners, or in any other matter, to try to put yourself on other people's level. If you are trying to do right, the chances are that, by adopting a coarse manner of speech or action, you will degrade yourself, and will fail in the good you seek. Rude and rough people are ready to excuse themselves for their own coarseness ; but, after all, they despise it in those who are striving to instruct and help them.

Cleanness and brightness and winsomeness, in thought and word and deed and manner and material surroundings, are always ready to help what is good. Coarseness and dinginess and ugliness are evils that must sometimes be endured, but ought never to be defended as virtues in themselve˙

---

## READY MEN.

READY MEN are generally witty men, and they are almost always talkative men. What Lord Bacon said two hundred years ago has never been contradicted. Reading makes a full man, conference a ready man, and writing an exact man, and accordingly, the nations that are most talkative are those that have most wit and most readiness. We count Lamb and Thackeray among the foremost of our humorists; but poor Elia, though matchless in the saying of good things, could rarely get them out fast, and Thackeray himself says that he thought of his own generally when he was in bed. With all his taste for society, he could never make a good after-dinner speech, and often envied Dickens his rare and valuable faculty. And yet he did in his life say some very good things. When he paid his first visit to America it was known of him that he was very fond of oysters, and, at a dinner given in his honor, the largest oyster that the place provided—quite an abnormal oyster, in point of size—was placed before him. He said himself that he turned pale when he saw it, but that he ate it in silence. His host asked him how he felt after, "Profoundly thankful," said Thackeray; "I feel as if I had swallowed a baby."

The rarest recorded instance of readiness was undoubtedly that of Foote, the comedian. He had given offence to a famous duellist of the day, who had vowed vengeance, and was only waiting to meet the luckless actor. Foote was told of it, and kept out of his way for a long time. At last they met at an inn where the actor generally dined, and where the duellist happened quite casually to come in. Foote saw his dan-

ger when it was too late; but, as his enemy said nothing, did his best to entertain him and keep him in
good humor.   No one could be more diverting when
he choose, and here he was not only very anxious but
very successful.   He told one story after another.   He
kept the table in a roar.   The fire-eater became quite
pacific, and was delighted with his new friend.   Foote
passed from one good story to another, and at last took
to imitating different people, a practice for which he
had extraordinary facility.   The other guests got quite
uproarious with the fun, when suddenly the luckless
actor saw from the face of his enemy that he had in-
advertently imitated one of his friends.   The duellist
was, in fact, putting his hand in his pocket to pull out
a card and present it as the preliminary to a challenge,
when he turned round to the mimic and said in a dry,
satiric voice, " Really, Mr. Foote, you are so uncom-
monly clever in taking other people off, I wonder
whether you could take yourself off." " Oh, certainly,"
said Foote, and he walked straightway into the street.
Here his readiness, probably, saved him his life.

It is noticeable how the characters of mind and
body correspond, and how the ready man is generally
quick in his movements, prompt in action and fertile
in resource.   The great Napoleon used to say that no
quality was so rare or so valuable as (what he called)

two-o'clock-in-the-morning courage. The power of suddenly changing front and altering the whole scheme of a campaign was precisely what the greatest of all modern strategists would admire. He himself eminently possessed it. The man who had the wit to say to the aristocrat who taunted him with his lack of ancestry, " *Moi, je suis ancetre,*" possessed a readiness of words as well as of action. He was not likely to lose either his head or his tongue. But this kind of promptitude is rarely coupled with staying power. It is distinctly meteoric, and part of the brilliancy is due to the gloom which follows it. And, therefore, the nations who most possess it are also purposeless, and without reserve of force.

---

## TIMELY JESTS.

MANY a promotion has been secured by a timely jest. The New York *Times* relates several of these happy "hits:"

Marshal Junot, while still a young subaltern, attracted the attention of the commander-in-chief by coolly observing, as an Austrian shell scattered earth over the despatch which he was writing, at the latter's dictation, "It's very kind of them to 'sand' our letters for us."

The traditions of the English navy have preserved another instance of the kind well worth quoting. When the Duke of Clarence, afterward William IV., went down to Portsmouth to inspect the British Seventy-fours, the guide allotted to him was a battered old lieutenant with one eye, who, lacking a " friend at court," had served for years without promotion.

As the veteran removed his hat to salute the royal visitor, the latter remarked his baldness, and said, jestingly, " I see my friend, you have not spared your hair in your country's service."

" Why, your Royal Highness," answered the old salt, " so many young fellows have stepped over my head that it's a wonder I have got any hair left."

The duke laughed loudly at this professional joke, but he made a note of the old man's name at the same time, and a few days after the latter received his appointment as captain.

---

## THE STEADY AND SOBER SUCCEED.

HOWEVER much people may propound to the contrary, the steady and sober men are to rise and be respected, while the dissolute and disorderly must sink and disappear. And though there is in many quarters a prejudice against piety—though some employers prefer workmen with easy principles and pliant consciences—no business can long prosper without probity, and no employer can become permanently rich with rogues for his servants. Hence, in all extensive and protracted undertakings, principle will undoubtedly win for itself an eventual preference; and the workman who understands his trade and keeps his character, may not only expect to keep his place, but perhaps become one day a partner in the establishment. If you won't tell a falsehood for your employer, neither will you waste his materials nor pilfer his property. And if you are not a sycophant in the slackest times, you will not be sauciest in the busiest; but, seeking first to please your Master in Heaven, you will find yourself rewarded with the goodwill and confidence of your superiors on earth.—*Hamilton.*

## COURAGE IN SICKNESS.

THE London *Lancet,* in a few words of good advice to sick people, says : " With the aid or under the influence of pluck, and using that term in a modern sense, and in relation to the daily heroism of life in the midst of difficulties, it is possible not only to surmount what appear to be insuperable

obstructions, but to defy and repel the ennuities of
climate, adverse circumstances, and even disease.
Many a life has been saved by the moral courage of a
sufferer. It is not alone in bearing the pain of operations or the misery of confinement in a sick-room, this
self-help becomes of vital moment, but in the monoto-
nous tracking of a weary path, and the vigorous discharge of ordinary duty. How many a victim of
incurable disease has lived on through years of suffering, patiently and resolutely hoping against hope, or,
what is better, living down despair, until the virulence
of a threatening malady has died out, and it has
ceased to he destructive, although its physical charac-
teristics remained?

"This power of 'good spirits' is a matter of high
moment to the sick and weakly. To the former it
may mean the ability to survive; to the latter, the
possibility of outliving, or living in spite of, a disease.
It is, therefore, of the greatest importance to cultivate
the highest and most buoyant frame of mind which
the conditions will admit. The same energy which
takes the form of mental activity is vital to the work
of the organism. Mental influences affect the system,
and a joyous spirit not only relieves pain, but increases
the momentum of life in the body.

"The multitude of healthy persons who wear out

their strength by exhaustive journeys and perpetual anxieties for health is very great, and the policy in which they indulge is exceedingly short-sighted. Most of the sorrowful and worried cripples who drag out miserable lives in this way, would be less wretched and live longer if they were more hopeful. It is useless to expect that anyone can be reasoned into a lighter frame of mind, but it is desirable that all should be taught to understand the sustaining, and often even curative power of 'good spirits.'"

---

## HOW TO READ.

IN answer to the question, How a young man shall read to the best advantage?—he should select some particular department of knowledge which he feels interesting, and within this department he should read carefully and studiously. If he only once make this selection, and make it rightly, other things will adjust themselves. He will not need very definite rules, nor will he need to concern himself about strict conformity with what rules he may have. The varied and desultory reading in which he may indulge will adapt itself in various ways to the main intellectual interest of his life. It will appropriate to its purpose the most stray information, while again the vivid central fire of his intellectual being will cast a light and meaning often around the most desultory particulars.

It may not seem easy to make such a choice; but every one more or less unconsciously makes it. The important matter is to recognize it to yourselves, and to build up your intellectual education upon it; because it can be really built up in no other manner. It is only by studying some particular subject with a view to mastering it, or some parts of it, that you can ever acquire a really studious insight and power. Nothing will enable you to realize your mental gifts, and to feel yourselves in the free and useful possession of them, like the triumph of bringing within your power and making your own some special subject.—*Abridged from Tulloch.*

## *WHAT TO READ.*

SOME books are to be tasted, others to be swallowed, and some few to be chewed and digested.

If this was true in Lord Bacon's time, how much more so is it in a time like ours, when books have multiplied beyond all precedent in the world's history.

It has become, in fact, a task beyond the power of any man to keep up, as it is said, with the rapidly-accumulating productions ·of literature, in all its branches. To enter a vast library, or even one of comparatively modest dimensions, such as all our large towns may boast, and survey the closely-packed shelves—the octavos rising above quartos, and duodecimos above both—is apt to fill the mind with a sense of oppression at the mere physical impossibility of ever coming in contact with such multiplied sources of knowledge. The old thought, *Ars longa, vita brevis*, comes home with a sort of sigh to the mind. Many lives would be wasted in the vain attempt. The inspection of a large library certainly cannot be recommended to inspire literary ambition. The names that shine in the horizon of fame are but specks amid the innumerable unknown that look down from the same eminence of repose.

Lord Macaulay has spoken especially of an "eminent soldier and distinguished diplomatist who has enjoyed the confidence of the first generals and statesmen which Europe has produced in our day," and who confessed that his success in life was mainly owing to his advantageous position when a young man, in the vicinity of a library. "When I asked to what he owed his accomplishments and success, he said to me,

'When I served when a young man in India—when it was the turning-point in my life—when it was a mere chance whether I should become a mere card-playing, hooka-smoking lounger—I was fortunately quartered for two years in the neighborhood of an excellent library, which was made accessible to me.' "

The influence of books at a certain stage of life is more than can be well estimated. The principles which they inculcate, the lessons which they exhibit, the ideals of life and character which they portray, root themselves in the thoughts and imaginations of young men. They seize them with a force which to after years appears scarcely possible. And when their faculties in mere restlessness might consume themselves in riotous frivolity and self-indulgence, they often receive in communion with some true and earnest book a right impulse which turns them to safety, happiness and honor.

The task of selection perhaps might be fairly left to individual taste and judgment.

Books may be classified conveniently enough in four divisions:

1. Philosophical and Theological.
2. Historical.
3. Scientific.
4. Books of Poetry and Fiction.

The young man in the full flush of his opening powers is naturally drawn to the examination and discussion of the highest problems that concern his being and happiness. There is a sanguine daring of speculation in the fresh and inexperienced mind which dashes at questions before which the veteran philosopher, warned by many defeats, sadly recoils. It may be often very useless in its results this youthful speculation, but, if not altogether misdirected, it may prove the most precious training. The mind rises, from its very defeats in such service, more vigorous and more elastic.

The great work of Locke on the "Human Understanding," every young man who has a love for speculation, ought to study; at any rate, he should master his small work on the "Conduct of the Understanding;" and to make even this little treatise his own thoroughly, and enter into all its meaning, he will find a most bracing and wholesome mental exercise.

A knowledge of theological literature is the business of the professed theologian. It can only be possible to others in rare circumstances. But every thinking man should know something of theology, and there are young minds that will by an irresistible impulse seek their main intellectual discipline in the reading of theological authors.

There are three great writers, each marking a century, we may say, of our past English theology, that may be very confidently recommended to the study of young men. These writers are Butler, Leighton, and Hooker. Butler, a master of theological argument, strong in logic, calm in spirit, comprehensive in aim. Leighton, like Pascal, a genius in religious meditation, deep, reflective, yet quick, sensitive, and tender—the *beau-ideal* of a Christian muser; never losing hold of the most practical duties in the most ethereal flights of his quaint and holy imagination. Hooker, a thinker of transcending compass, sweeping in the range of his imperial mind the whole circumference of Christian speculation—rising with the wings of boldness to the heights of the Divine government, and yet folding them with the sweetest reverence before the Throne. There are many other great names in English theological literature, but there are none greater than these.

Every young man should give his earnest attention to the reading of Scripture. Let him not suppose that he can easily know all that it contains. Let him not be contented to read a chapter now and then, rather as a duty than as a living interest and education. No reading should be so interesting to him ; none, certainly, can form to him so high an education. It is

not only his Christian intelligence and sensibility that
will be everywhere drawn forth in the perusal of its
blessed pages, but his taste, his imagination and reason
will be exercised and regaled in the highest degree.
Its poetry is, beyond all other poetry, incomparable,
not only in the height of its Divine arguments, as
Milton suggests, but in "the very critical art of com-
position." Its narratives are models of simplicity and
graphic life. It abounds in almost every species of
literary excellence and intellectual sublimity. It is,
above all, the inspired Word of God—the source of all
spiritual truth and illumination. Whatever you read,
therefore, do not forget to read the Bible. Let it be
as the "man of your counsel, and the guide of your
right hand," as a "light to your feet, and a lantern to
your path." "The law of the Lord is perfect, con-
verting the soul; the testimony of the Lord is sure,
making wise the simple; the statutes of the Lord are
right, rejoicing the heart; the commandment of the
Lord is pure, enlightening the eyes." "Wherewithal
shall a young man cleanse his way? By taking heed
thereto according to thy word."

Of the many great historical works which our age
has produced, there are some so popular and universally read that it is needless to recommend them.
Macaulay's wonderful volumes, as they successively

8

appeared, carried captive the minds of old and young.

The works of Hallam, of Thirlwall and Grote, of Milman and Prescott, of Froude and of Motley, show in their mere enumeration what a field lies before the student here. The careful study of any one of these histories is an education in itself; and there is no mental task could be recommended as more appropriate and more valuable to the young man. To read them as a whole is never an easy matter; and it will be found, in point of fact, they are but rarely read and studied so completely as they ought to be. The young man cannot brace himself to any higher effort, or one more likely to tell upon his whole intellectual life. The study of such works as we have mentioned, or of many others that might be mentioned—Clarendon's graphic pages—Gibbon's magnificent drama—may serve to date an epoch in his educational development. Many can recall how the perusal of such a masterpiece as Gibbon's "Decline and Fall of the Roman Empire" served to raise the conception of what the human mind could do, and left an indelible impress on the intellectual character.

In studying such works the aim should be to master them, and if possible their subject, so thoroughly as to be able to exercise a free judgment as to what you read. To read merely that you may repeat the views of the historian, or perhaps imbibe his prejudices, is a poor and even an injurious result. You must read rather that you may understand his subject; and if he is really a great historian, he will enable you to do this to some extent independently of his own representations. Using his pages, you must yet look through them, and endeavor to realize the course of facts for yourself. Especially aim, by an active sympathy and intelligent perception of what is going on around you—of the history that is being daily wrought out under your eyes and in your own experience—to get some living apprehension of the past, some real understanding of its great events and characters, its social manners, its laws, institutions, and modes of government, the condition of the people in their different ranks and relations, the interior of their family life, their diet, their industry, and their amusements. It is but recently that historians have recognized the necessity of treating some of these topics, but it is becoming more and more evident that it is such topics, and not the mere details of battles or of royal doings, that form the real staple of history. Whatever contributes to unveil the past, to make it an intelligible reality and not a mere shadowy picture, is the right material of history; and its highest use is to give such an insight into the past as may happily guide and influence the future.

Of all departments of knowledge, indeed, that of popular science may be said to be making the most advance.

Sir John Herschel, Sir David Brewster, Hugh Miller, Mr. Lewes, Mr. Hunt, and others, have all written of science so as to interest any but the most indifferent minds. And the young student who would follow out such studies will find in the writings of these well-known authors at once their plainest and their highest guides. Such works as those of Hugh Miller on geology, and Mr. Lewes's " Sea-side Studies," and Professor Johnston's " Chemistry of Common Life," and Mr. Faraday's " Lectures for the Young," not to mention others, show how numerously books lie to his hand in this department of study.

In such studies let it be your aim not merely to accumulate facts, nor store your memories with details, but also to grasp principles. It is from lack of doing this that many minds turn away in weariness from scientific pursuits.

Youthful study advances under a spur of poetic enthusiasm more than anything else. Carry this enthusiasm with you into the study of nature. Learn to appreciate its beauties, to admire its harmonies, as you explore its secrets. This is surely the natural result that should follow an increased acquaintance with scientific facts. The more nature is studied, the more should all its poetry appear.

Books of Poetry and Fiction are the last class that we have enunciated. In many respects they are the most important.

Looking to the moral effect of our modern poetry and fiction upon the young, there is nothing more deserving of commendation than the increased spirit of human sympathy for which they are remarkable. The literature of the last age was especially defective in this respect. It lacked genial tenderness or earnest sympathy for human suffering and wrong. Its very pathos was hard and artificial. It wept over imaginary sorrows; it rejoiced in merely sentimental triumphs. In contrast to this, the poetry and fiction of our time concern themselves closely with the common sorrows and joys of the human heart. The pages of Dickens and Kingsley, and Miss Mulock and Mrs. Gaskell, and Mrs. Oliphant and George Eliot, are all intensely realistic. A deep-thoughted tenderness for human miseries, and a high aspiration after human improvement, animate all of them. It is impossible to read their novels without having our moral sentiments acutely touched and drawn forth. The same is eminently true of the poetry of Mr. Tennyson, Mrs. Browning, and others. It is almost more than anything characterized by a spirit of impassioned philanthropy, of intense yearning over worldly wrong and error, "ancient forms of party strife," and of lofty longing after a higher good than the world has yet known—

> " Sweeter manners, purer laws,
> The larger heart, the kindlier hand."

It is impossible for the young to love such poetry and to study it without a kindling in them of something of the same affectionate interest in human welfare and aspiration after human improvement.

Of course, they will read what is most popular and interesting. There is one writer, however, neither a poet nor a novelist, and yet in some respects both, whom we feel urged to commend to their study—the author of "Friends in Council," "Essays written in the Intervals of Business," and " Companions of my Solitude," etc. These volumes are charming, at once for their literary finish, their genial earnestness, and their thoughtful, ethical spirit.

We should further urge upon young men the necessity of extending their studies in the lighter departments of literature beyond their own age. They must and will reap mainly, as we have supposed, the fiction and poetry of their time, but in order to get any adequate culture from this sort of reading they must do something more. They must study English poetry in its successive epochs, ascending by such stages as are represented by the great names of Wordsworth, and Cowper, and Dryden, and Milton, and Shakspeare, and Spenser. To study thoroughly the great works of any of these poets, especially of Wordsworth, or Milton, or Shakspeare, or Spenser, is a lasting educational gain. Any youth who spends his leisure over the pages of the " Excursion," or the " Paradise Lost," or the " Fairy Queen," or the higher dramas of Shakspeare, is engaged in an important course of intellectual discipline. And if you would wish to know the charms of literary delight in their full freedom and acquisition, you must have often recourse to these great lights of literature, and seek to kindle your love for " whatsoever hath passion or admiration " at the flame of their genius.

Altogether it is evident what a wide field of study is before every young man who loves books, and would seek to improve himself by their study. The field is only too wide and varied, were it not that different tastes will seek different parts of it, and leave the rest comparatively alone. Whatever part you may select, devote yourself to it. If history, or science, or belles lettres be your delight, read with a view not merely to pass the time, but really to cultivate and advance your intellectual life.   The mere dilettante will never come to anything.   Read whatever you read with enthusiasm, with a generous yet critical sympathy.   Make it your own.   Take it up by lively and intelligent application at every point into your own mental system, and assimilate it.   An active interest is a condition of all mental improvement.   The mind only expands or strengthens when it is fairly awakened. Give to all your reading an awakened attention, a mind alive and hungering after knowledge, and whether you read history, or poetry, or science, or theology, or even fiction of a worthy kind, it will prove to you a mental discipline, and bring you increase of wisdom. —*Abridged from Tulloch.*

## *HOW TO ENJOY.*

EVERY life that is at all healthy and happy must have its enjoyments as well as its duties.   It cannot bear the constant strain of grave occupation without losing something of its vitality and sinking into feebleness. Asceticism may have construed life as an unceasing routine of duty—of work done for some grave or solemn purpose.  But asceticism has

neither produced the best work nôr the noblest lives
of which our world can boast. In its effort to elevate
human nature, it has risen at the highest to a barren
grandeur. It has too often relapsed into moral weakness or perversity. Human nature, as a prime condition of health, must recreate itself—must have its
moments of unconscious play, when it throws off the
burden of work, and rejoices in the mere sensation of
its own free activity.

And youth must especially have such opportunities
of recreation. It thirsts for them—it is all on the alert
to catch them ; and if denied to it, it dwindles from
its proper strength, or pursues illegitimate and hurtful
gratifications. A young man without the love of
amusement is an unnatural phenomenon ; and an
education that does not provide for recreation as well
as study would fail of its higher end from the very ex-
clusiveness with which it aims to reach it.

The question, How to enjoy? is therefore, in its
right sense, always a secondary, never a primary question. It comes after the question of duty, and never
before it; and where the main question is rightly
resolved, the secondary one becomes comparatively
easy of solution. Principle first: Play afterwards.
And if there be the root of right principle in us, we
will not, need not trouble ourselves minutely as to

modes of amusement.   Enjoyment in itself is meant to
be a right and blessing, and not a snare.   This is a
very important truth for the young to understand.
Life is open to them; amusement is free to them.
They are entitled to live freely and trustfully, and enjoy
all—if only the sense of duty and of God remain with
them—if only they do not forget that for all these things
God will bring them into judgment.   Under this proviso
they may taste of enjoyment as liberally as their
natures crave, and their opportunities offer.   To preach
anything else to the young, is neither true in itself nor
can possibly be good to them.   To teach them to be
afraid of enjoyment, is to make them doubtful of
their own natural and healthy instincts ; and as these
instincts remain, nevertheless, and constantly reassert
their power, it is to introduce an element of hurtful
perplexity into their life.   They are urged on by
nature ; they are held back by authority.   And if the
rein of the outward law imposed upon them once
break, they are plunged into darkness.   They have no
guide.   It is vain to enter into this struggle with
nature : it is cruel and wrong to do it.   Nature must
have play, and is to be kept within bounds by its own
wise training, and the development of a higher spirit
within, and not by mere dictation and arbitrary com-
pulsion from without.

Ascetic formality is the refuge of a weak moral nature, or the wretchedness of a strong one. How far even a noble mind may sink under it—to what depths of despairing imbecility and almost impiety it may reach—we have only to study the austerities of Pascal to see. We are told that "Pascal would not permit himself to be conscious of the relish of his food; he prohibited all seasonings and spices, however much he might wish for and need them; and he actually died because he forced the diseased stomach to receive at each meal a certain amount of aliment, neither more nor less, whatever might be his appetite at the time, or his utter want of appetite. He wore a girdle armed with iron spikes, which he was accustomed to drive in upon his body (his fleshless ribs) as often as he thought himself in need of such admonition. He was annoyed and offended if any in his hearing might chance to say that they had just seen a beautiful woman. He rebuked a mother who permitted her own children to give her their kisses. Towards a loving sister, who devoted herself to his comfort, he assumed an artificial harshness of manner for the *express purpose*, as he acknowledged, of revolting her sisterly affection."

And all this sprung from the simple principle that earthly enjoyment was inconsistent with religion.

Once admit this principle, and there is no limit to the abject and unhappy consequences that may be drawn from it. The mind, thrown off any dependence upon its own instincts, is cast into the arms of some blind authority or dogmatism which tyrannizes over it, reducing it more frequently to weakness than bracing it up to endurance and heroism.

No doubt it will be the impulse of every Christian man, and it ought no less to be so of every Christian youth, to "rejoice with trembling." While he hears the voice saying to him, on the one hand, "Rejoice, O young man, in thy youth, and let thy heart cheer thee in the days of thy youth, and walk in the ways of thine heart, and in the sight of thine eyes;" he will not forget the voice that says to him, on the other hand, "But know thou, that for all these things God will bring thee into judgment." The voices are one, in fact; and if he is wise, he will acknowledge their unity, and be sober in his very mirth, and temper the hour of cheerfulness with the thought of responsibility. There is something in the heart itself, even in the heart of the young, that intimates this as the true mean. There is often a monition of warning in the very moment of mirth. The joy is well. It is the natural expression of a healthy and well-ordered frame; it leaps up to meet the opportunity as the lark to greet the morn. The movement of nature is as clear in the one case as in the other; yet there is a background of moral consciousness lying behind the human instinct, and always ready to cast the shadows of thought—of reflective responsibility over it.

Our constitution contains within itself a check to all undue excitement. This check is, no doubt, often ineffectual, but it is so at the expense of the constitution, and the very capacity of enjoyment which may overtask itself. This capacity wastes by excessive use. Of nothing may the young man be more sure than this. If he will rejoice without thought and without care in the days of his youth, he will leave but little power of enjoyment for his manhood or old age. If he keep the flame of passion burning, and plunge into excitement after excitement in his heyday, there will be nothing but feebleness and exhaustion in his maturity. He cannot spend his strength and have it too. He cannot drink of every source of pleasure, and have his taste uncloyed, and his thirst fresh as at the first.

There is need here of a special caution in a time like ours. There are young men who now-a-days exhaust pleasure in their youth. The comparative freedom of modern life encourages an earlier entrance into the world, and an earlier assᵗ mption of manly manners and habits than was wont to be. Pleasure is cheaper and more accessible—the pleasure of travel, pleasure of many kinds; and it is no uncommon thing to find young men who have run the round of manly pleasure before they have well attained to man's estate, and who are *blasé* with the world before the time that their fathers had really entered into it.

The avoidance of all excess is a golden rule in enjoyment. It may be a hard, and in certain cases an impossible rule to the young. In the abundance of life there is a tendency to overflow; and when the young heart is big with excited emotion it seems vain to speak of moderation. Every one, probably, will be able to recall hours when, amid the competitive gladness of school or college companions the impulses of enjoyment seemed to burst all bounds, and ran into the most riotous excitement; and in the reminiscences of such hours there may be the charm as of a long-lost pleasure never to be felt again; but if the memory be fairly interrogated, it will be found that even then there was a drawback—some latent dissatisfaction and weariness, or something worse, that grew out of the very height or overplus of that rapturous enjoyment. As a great humorist (Thomas Hood) has said:

> " E'en the bright extremes of joy
> Bring on conclusions of disgust."

Assuredly the most durable and the best pleasures are
all tranquil pleasures. And it is just one of the lessons which change the sanguine anticipations of youth
into the sober experience of manhood that the true
essence of attainable enjoyment is not in bursts of
excitement, but in the moderate flow of healthy and
happy, because well-ordered, emotion.—*Abridged from
Tulloch.*

## WHAT TO ENJOY.

YOUTH must have its recreations. Enjoyment
must mingle largely in the life of every healthy
young man—enjoyment liberal yet temperate.
The active sports of boyhood may be, and as far as
possible should be, carried into early manhood.
Athletic games, or whatever game carries the young
man into the open air, braces his muscles, and
strengthens his health, and procures the merry-hearted
companionship of his fellows, should be indulged in
without stint, so far as his opportunities will permit,
and the proper claims of business or of study justify.

There is another class of amusements to which
young men may freely betake themselves as they have
opportunity—shooting and fishing.

In addition to such out-door amusements, there are

various forms of in-door amusement which claim some notice. It is more difficult to find in-door amusements for young men, for the simple reason that healthy and happy exercise is the idea which is chiefly associated with, and chiefly legitimates recreation on their part. And the open air is the natural place for such exercise. Yet in-door amusements must also be found. Music is one of the chief of these amusements, and certainly one of the most innocent and elevating.

Of all delights, to those who have the gift or taste for it, music is the most exquisite. To affix the term amusement to it is perhaps scarcely fair. It is always more than this when duly appreciated.

There is no other recreation, if this be the proper name for it at all, which is so purely intellectual. Other amusements, many games, may exercise the intellect, and even largely draw forth its powers of forethought, of decision and readiness; but music appeals to the soul in those deeper springs which lie close to spiritual and moral feeling. It lifts it out of the present and visible into the future and invisible. Even in its gayer and lighter strains it often does this, as well as in its more solemn and sacred chants. The simple lilt of a song which we have heard in youth, or which reminds us of home and country—some fragment of melody slight in meaning, yet exquisitely touching in sweet or pathetic wildness—will carry the soul into a higher region, and make a man feel kindred with the immortals.

> " O joy! that in our embers
> Is something that doth live;
> That nature yet remembers
> What was so fugitive!"

A joy so precious as this, and which may minister to such high ends, is one which we are bound to cultivate in every manner, and for which we are warranted in seeking the fullest indulgence. The concert, the oratorio, the opera, are all, from this point of view, to be commended.

The love of *play* of any kind in the shape of billiards or cards, or anything else, is a hazardous, and may prove, before you are well aware of it, a fatal passion. Whenever it begins to develop, you have passed the bounds of amusement; and to indulge in any games but for amusement is at once an infatuation and temptation of the worst kind.

The drama is in its idea noble and exalting—one of the most natural, and therefore most effective expressions of literary art. Who may not be made wiser and better by the study of Shakspeare's wonderful creations? In what human compositions rather than in his plays would a young man seek for the stimulus of high thoughts, and the excitement of lofty and

9

heroic or gentle and graceful virtues? The stage in its true conception is a school of morals as well as of manners, in which the things that are excellent should commend themselves, and the things that are low and bad show their own disgrace. There is no species of entertainment that can, according to its true idea, more completely vindicate itself than the theatre.

Festive parties among yourselves, how light and genial may they be! What feast of reason and flow of soul! What flash of wit and cannonade of argument may they call forth! What radiant sparks, the memory of which will never die out, but come back in the easy and humorous moments of an earnest and it may be a sad existence, and brighten up the past with the momentary coruscations of a departed brilliancy! What deep, hearty friendship may illuminate and beautify them! Yet we know that such gladsome moments are peculiarly akin to danger. Merriment may pass into wantonness, and legitimate indulgence into a riotous carouse. Moderation is the difficulty of youth in everything. Yet when the bounds of moderation are once passed, all the enjoyment is gone—recreation ceases. Edward Irving says:

" Mirth and laughter, and the song, and the dance, and the feast, and the wine-cup, with all the jovial glee which circulates around the festive board, are only proper to the soul at those seasons when she is filled with extraordinary gladness, and should wait until those seasons arrive in order to be partaken of wholesomely and well; but by artificial means to make an artificial excitement of the spirits is violently to change the law and order of our nature, and to force it to that to which it is not willingly inclined. Without such high calls and occasions, to make mirth and laughter is to belie nature, and misuse the ordinance of God. It is a false glare, which doth but show the darkness and deepen the gloom. It is to wear out and dissipate the oil of gladness, so that, when gladness cometh, we have no light of joy within our souls, and look upon it with baleful eyes. It is not a figure, but a truth, that those who make those artificial merriments night after night, have no taste for natural mirth, and are gloomy and morose until the revels of the table or the lights of the saloon bring them to life again. Nature is worsted by art—artificial fire is stolen, but not from heaven, to quicken the pulse of life, and the pulse of life runs on with fevered speed, and the strength of man is prostrated in a few brief years, and old age comes over the heart when life should yet be in its prime. And not only is heaven made shipwreck of, but the world is made shipwreck of—not only the spiritual man quenched, but the

animal man quenched, by such unseasonable and intemperate merrymakings."

In all your enjoyments, therefore, be moderate.
The principle that leads and regulates you must be
from within.   Set your heart right in the love of God
and the·faith of Christ, and difficulties will disappear.
Your recreation will fit in naturally to your life.   The
inner life in you will assimilate to the Divine everywhere, and return its own blessed and consecrating
influence to all your work and all your amusments.—
*Abridged from Tulloch.*

---

## *MARRIAGE.*

HE foundation of every good government is the
family.  The best and most prosperous country
is that which has the greatest number of happy
firesides.   The holiest institution among men is marriage.   It has taken the race countless ages to come up
to the condition of marriage.   Without it there would
be no civilization, no human advancement, no life
worth living.   Life is a failure to any woman who has
not secured the love and adoration of some grand and
magnificent man.   Life is a mockery to any man, no
matter whether he be mendicant or monarch, who has

not won the heart of some worthy woman. Without love and marriage, all the priceless joys of this life would be as ashes on the lips of the children of men.

"You had better be the emperor of one loving and tender heart, and she the empress of yours, than to be the king of the world. The man who has really won the love of one good woman in this world, it matters not though he die in the ditch a beggar, his life has been a success."

There is a heathen book which says: "Man is strength, woman is beauty; man is courage, woman is love. When the one man loves the one woman, and the one woman loves the one man, the very angels leave heaven and come and sit in that house and sing for joy."—*The Physiologist.*

---

## WHY A MAN NEEDS A WIFE.

IT is not to sweep the house, make the bed, darn the socks and cook the meals chiefly, that a man wants a wife. If this is all he needs, hired help can do it cheaper than a wife. If this is all, when a young man calls to see a lady, send him into the pantry to taste the bread and cake she has made; send him to inspect the needlework and bed-making; or put a broom in her hand, and send him to witness its use. Such things are important, and the wise young man will quickly look after them ; but what the true man wants with a wife is her companionship, sympathy and love. The way of life has many dreary places in it, and man needs a companion to go with him. A man is sometimes overtaken by misfortune ; he meets with failure and defeat ; trials and temptations beset him, and he needs one to stand by and sympathize. He has some hard battles to fight with poverty, enemies, and with sin ; and he needs a woman that, when he puts his arm around her, he feels he has something to fight for, she will help him to fight. All through life, through storms and through sunshine, conflict and victory ; through adverse and through favoring winds, man needs a woman's love. Happy he who finds it.

## HAPPINESS.

EVER since the world sinned and woke up to misery, there is one absentee whom all have agreed in deploring. Every age has asked tidings of her from the age that has went before, and from the one which came after; and even the most indolent have put forth an effort, and have joined their neighbors in searching for this fugitive. Some have dived into the billowy main, and sought her in pearly grottoes and coral caves. And some have bored into the solid rock, and rummaged for her in the mountain roots. And some have risen to where the eagles poise, and have scanned in successive horizons the habitable surface; but all have got the same report. "Where is happiness?"—"Not in me," cries the leafy grove; "nor in me," booms the sounding tide; "nor in me," rumbles gaunt and hollow from the dusky mine. And failing to detect her in life's by-paths and open ways, her votaries have reared decoys or shrines into which she haply might turn aside. But all of them have failed entirely. Theatres, dancing-saloons, gin-palaces, racing-booths—there is no authentic instance that she ever entered one of them. And though some have fancied that they glimpsed her—"yes, yes," they whisper, "yonder she passed; and in that hall of science, in that temple of knowledge, in that sweet home, you'll find her;" by the time you reached it, there was a death's-head at the door, and a "Mene Tekel" on the wall. "Not in me," sighed vain philosophy; and "not in me," re-echoed the worldling's rifled home.

But where is happiness? Man knows that she is not dead, but disappeared; and ever since under the forbidden tree he ate the bitter-sweet and startled her away, he has longed to find that other and enlightening fruit which would reveal her to his eyes again. And this is the boon which the world's teachers have undertaken to supply. They have come from time to time, seers and sages, Thales, Pythagoras, Zoroaster, Epicurus, Con-fu-tze, and to humanity's wondering gaze they have held up apples, as they said, fresh gathered from the Tree of Life. But after rushing and jostling round them, and getting at great cost a prize, these all proved naught to the hungry buyer. The golden apples were mere make-believes; hollow rinds, painted shells filled up with trash or trifles. Some ate, and still their soul had appetite; others ate, and were poisoned.

At last, along the path which a hundred prophecies had carved and smoothed, "the desire of all nations" —the Son of God—appeared. And from the paradise above he fetched the long-lost secret. Himself "the truth;" his every sentence freighted with majesty, and fragrant with heaven's sanctity; it needed not the frequent miracle to compel the exclamation, " Rabbi, we know that thou art a teacher come from God." He did not reason ; he revealed. His sayings were not the conjectures of keen sagacity, nor even the recollections of an angel visitor; but they were authoritative words—the insight of Omniscience, the oracle of in-carnate Deity. And giving freely to all comers "the apples of gold" from his "basket of silver," the dim and the famished ate, and with open eyes looking up, in himself they recognized the answer to the ancient query. "What is happiness?"—"Come unto me," is the Saviour's reply; "come unto me, all ye that labor and are heavy laden, and I will give you rest. Take my yoke upon you, and learn of me; for I am meek and lowly in heart: and ye shall find rest unto your souls." "Where is happiness?" Here, at the feet of Immanuel. And then, and since, thousands have veri-fied the saying. In the words of Jesus they have dis-covered the boon for which their understandings longed—conclusive and soul-filling knowledge; and in his person and work they have found the good for which their conscience craved—a saving and sanctify-ing Power.

To the great question, What is happiness? Jesus is the embodied answer—at once the teacher and the les-son. The question had been asked for ages, and some hundred solutions had been proposed. And in the outset of his ministry the Saviour took it up, and gave the final answer. What is happiness? "Happy are the humble. Happy are the contrite. Happy are the meek. Happy are they who hunger after righteousness.  Happy are the merciful, the pure in heart, the peace-makers, the men persecuted for righteousness." In other words, he declared that happiness is goodness.  A holy nature is a happy one.

Placed before you is a casket of gold, and you are asked to guess what it contains; and looking at its exquisite tracery and costly material, you think of a blazing diamond or a monarch's signet-ring.  Guess? You can not guess.  They open it, and reveal a spider, a scorpion, or a spinning-worm!  And surveying a human soul, you view the finest casket in this world. Made on a heavenly pattern, with powers so capacious, and feelings so susceptible, in order to be worthily occupied, it would need to be filled with some lofty purpose, some pure and noble motive.  My reader, you have got that casket.  What have you put in it ? What is the thing which chiefly occupies your thoughts? Your great pursuit and pleasure?  What impels you to exertion?  Is it money?  Is it popularity and praise? Is it dress?  Is it dainty food?  Is it some fierce and evil passion?  Is it envy?  Is it resentment?  Is it selfishness?  Is it the wish to achieve your own personal ease and comfort?  Is it something so paltry that you are ashamed to call it the business of life?—something so baleful that it degrades and destroys the heart which hides it?

Seek to have your bosom filled with pure kindness and holy compassion—a compassion various as is human sorrow—a kindness which shall still be flowing while life itself is ebbing. Cease to be selfish. Learn the blessedness of doing good. Even you can contribute to that great work—the making of a bad world better. Is there no acquaintance over whom you have influence? None whom you might reclaim from a bad habit? None whom you might induce to read some useful book, or attend the house of God? Are there no poor children whom you might collect on a Sabbath afternoon, and teach them a Bible lesson? Is there no sick neighbor to whom you might carry a little comfort—something nice to tempt his listless palate? No invalid friend whom you might cheer with an hour of your company, or to whom you might read or say something for the good of his soul? At all events, you can be doing good at home. You can minister to the wants of some aged parent. You can sooth the grief of some bereaved relation. You can lend a helping hand, and lighten their labors who have got too much to do. With a firm but fatherly control, you can guide your children in wisdom's ways. And you can diffuse throughout your dwelling that sweetest music—cheerful and approving words; that brightest light—the clear shining of a cordial countenance.

And when God in His Providence sends favorable opportunities, with self-denial and prayerful affection, you may be the means of stamping on some immortal mind a truth or lesson as enduring as that mind itself.

You will not need to study your appearance, nor to be nervous about people's opinions; for by its self-sustaining sincerity, your conduct will sooner or later achieve its own vindication, and in her child shall Wisdom be justified. In your common talk there will be no scurrility nor scandal; nothing false, nothing unseemly, nothing base nor vile. In your ordinary acting, there will be no crooks nor crotchets; nothing cruel or oppressive; nothing for which conscience can not render a good reason.—*Hamilton.*

———

## SUCCESS

WHETHER your life shall be successful or not, is a question which must be answered by yourself alone. It cannot be done by proxy. Temperance, frugality, honesty, and economy, accompanied by strong determination and perseverance, will bring you to the goal of success and prosperity. Nothing else will. "The longer I live," said Fowell Buxton, "the more I am certain that the great difference between men, between the feeble and the powerful, the great and the insignificant, is *energy—invincible determination*—a purpose once fixed, and then death or victory! That quality will do anything that can be done in this world; and no talents, no circumstances, no opportunities, will make a two-legged creature a man without it." The path of success in business is invariably the path of common sense. The best kind of success in every man's life is not that which comes by accident, and "lucky hits" often turn out very unlucky in the end. "We may succeed for a time by fraud, by surprise, by violence; but we can succeed permanently only by means directly opposite." "Honesty is the best policy," and it is upheld by the daily experience of life; uprightness and integrity being found as successful in business as in everything else. It is possible that the scrupulously honest man may not grow rich so fast as the unscrupulous and dishonest one; but the success will be of a truer kind, earned without fraud or injustice. And even though a man should for a time be unsuccessful, still he must be honest; better lose all and save character. For character is itself a fortune, and if the high-principled man will but hold in his way courageously, success will surely come—nor will the highest reward of all be withheld from him.

The rules of conduct followed by Lord Erskine are worthy of being engraven on every young man's heart: "It was a first command and counsel of my earliest youth," he said, "always to do what my conscience told me to be a duty, and to leave the consequence to God. I shall carry with me the memory, and I trust the practice, of this parental lesson, to the grave. I have hitherto followed it, and I have no reason to complain that my obedience to it has been a temporal sacrifice. I have found it, on the contrary, the road to prosperity and wealth, and I shall point out the same path to my children for their pursuit."

Disappointments and difficulties may fall to your lot, but let them not crush your determination to succeed. George Stephenson worked fifteen years at the improvement of his locomotive before achieving his decisive victory. William Cobbett mastered English grammar when a private soldier on the pay of sixpence a day, and often underwent great hardship in his efforts to advance in knowledge. Audubon, the ornithologist, had two hundred of his original drawings, representing two thousand inhabitants of air, eaten up by rats, and the loss nearly put a stop to his researches. He took up his gun, note-book and pencils, and went forth to the woods gayly, as if nothing had happened. In three years his portfolio was again filled. The list of men who have overcome what seemed to others insurmountable obstacles is a long one, and the few instances given are sufficient to illustrate the power of determination and perseverance. " What is even poverty itself," asks Richter, " that a man should murmur under it ? It is but as the pain of piercing a maiden's ear, and you hang precious jewels in the wound." Many are found capable of bravely bearing up under privations and trials, who are afterwards found unable to withstand the more dangerous influences of prosperity. Prosperity is apt to harden the heart to pride; adversity, in a man of resolution, will only serve to ripen it to fortitude. Difficulties may intimidate the weak, but they act only as a wholesome stimulus to men of pluck and resolution. All experience of life, indeed, serves to prove that the impediments thrown in the way of success may, for the most part, be overcome by steady conduct, honest zeal, activity, perseverance, and above all, by a determined resolution to surmount difficulties, and stand up manfully against misfortune.

"Honor and shame from no condition rise,
Act well your part, there all the honor lies."

Be it yours to strive and win, and to obtain in this world riches and honor, and in the world to come a " crown of life." Such a victory is surely the greatest success that can be attained, and is far more lasting and enduring than so-called success obtained by fraud and trickery, however much it may appear to the contrary at times.

———

There are many who, in their eager desire for the end, overlook the difficulties in the way; there is another class who see nothing else. The first class may sometimes fail; the latter rarely succeed.

———

## THE IRREPARABLE PAST.

TIME is the solemn inheritance to which every man is born heir, who has a life-rent of this world—a little section cut out of eternity, and given us to do our work in; an eternity before, an eternity behind: and the small stream between, floating swiftly from the one into the vast bosom of the other. The man who has felt, with all his soul, the significance of time, will not be long in learning any lesson that this world has to teach him. Have you ever felt it? Have you ever realized how your own little streamlet is gliding away and bearing you along with it towards that awful other world of which all things here are but thin shadows, down into that eternity towards which the confused wreck of all earthly things is bound ?

Let us realize, that, until that sensation of time, and the infinite meaning which is wrapped up in it, has taken possession of our souls, there is no chance of our ever feeling strongly that it is worse than madness to sleep that time away. Every day in this world has its work; and every day, as it rises out of eternity, keeps putting to each of us the question afresh, What will you do before to-day has sunk into eternity and nothingness again?

And now what have we to say with respect to this strange, solemn thing—TIME? That men do with it through life just what the Apostles did for one precious and irreparable hour of it in the garden of Geth-semane—they go to sleep! Have you ever seen those marble statues, in some public square or garden, which art has so finished into a perennial fountain that through the lips or through the hands the clear water flows in a perpetual stream on and on forever, and the marble stands there—passive, cold—making no effort to arrest the gliding water?

It is so that time flows through the hands of men—swift, never pausing till it has run itself out; and there is the man petrified into a marble sleep, not feeling what it is which is passing away forever! It is so, just

so, that the destiny of nine men out of ten accomplishes itself, slipping away from them aimless, useless,
till it is too late. And we are asked, with all the
solemn thoughts which crowd around our approaching
eternity, What has been our life, and what do we in-
tend it shall be ?

Yesterday, last week, last year, they are gone! Yesterday was such a day as never was before, and never
can be again. Out of darkness and eternity it was
born, a new, fresh day; into darkness and eternity it
sank again forever. It had a voice, calling to us of
its own—its own work, its own duties. What were we
doing yesterday? Idling, whiling away the time, in
light and luxurious literature; not as life's relaxation,
but as life's business? Thrilling our hearts with the
excitement of life, contriving how to spend the day
most pleasantly? Was that our day?

All this is but the sleep of the three Apostles. And
now let us remember this: There is a day coming
when the sleep will be broken rudely—with a shock;
there is a day in our future lives when our time will
be counted, not by years, nor by months, nor yet by
hours, but by minutes—the day when unmistakabie
symptoms shall announce that the messenger of death
has come to take us.

That startling moment will come, which it is vain to

attempt to realize now, when it will be felt that it is all over at last—that our chance and our trial are past. The moment that we have tried to think of, shrunk from, put away from us, here it is—going too, like all other moments that have gone before it; and then with eyes unsealed at last, we shall look back on the life which is gone by.—*Robertson.*

## PREPARE FOR THE END.

IT is well for the young man, even in entering upon life, to remember its termination, and how swiftly and suddenly the end may come. "Here we have no continuing city." We are "strangers and pilgrims, as all our fathers were," and the road of life at its very opening may pass from under us, and ere we have well entered upon the enjoyments and work of the present, we may be launched into the invisible and future world that awaits us. At the best life is but a brief space. "It appeareth for a little moment, and then vanisheth away." It is but a flash out of darkness, soon again to return into darkness. Or, as the old Saxon imagination conceived, it is like the swift flight of a bird from the night without, through a lighted chamber, filled with guests and warm with the

breath of passion, back into the cold night again
(Bede, ii., 13). We stand, as it were, on a narrow
"strip of shore, waiting till the tide, which has washed
away hundreds of millions of our fellows, shall wash
us away also into a country of which there are no
charts, and from which there is no return." The
image may be almost endlessly varied. The strange
and singular uncertainty of life is a stock theme of
pathos; but no descriptive sensibility can really touch
all the mournful tenderness which it excites.

It is not easy for a young man, nor indeed for any
man in high health and spirits, to realize the transi-
toriness of life and all its ways. Nothing would be
less useful than to fill the mind with gloomy images of
death, and to torment the present by apprehensions
as to the future. Religion does not require nor
countenance any such morbid anxiety; yet it is good
also to sober the thoughts with the consciousness of
life's frailty and death's certainty. It is good above
all to live every day as we would wish to have done
when we come to die. We need not keep the dread
event before us, but we should do our work and duty
as if we were ever waiting for it and ready to encounter it. "Whatsoever thy hand findeth to do, do it
with thy might; for there is no work, nor device, nor
knowledge, nor wisdom in the grave, whither thou

goest." Our work here should always be preparatory for the end. Our enjoyments should be such as shall not shame us when we stand face to face with death. The young, and the old too, but especially the young, are apt to forget this. In youth we fail to realize the intimate dependency, the moral coherency which binds life together everywhere, and gives an awful meaning to every part of it. We do not think of consequences as we recklessly yield to passion, or stain the soul by sinful indulgence. But the storm of passion never fails to leave its waste, and the stain, although it may have been washed by the tears of penitence, and the blood of a Saviour, remains. There is something different, something less firm, less clear, honest, or consistent in our life in consequence; and the buried sin rises from its grave in our sad moments, and haunts us with its terror, or abashes us with its shame. Assuredly it will find us out at last, if we lose not all spiritual sensibility. When our feet begin "to stumble on the dark mountains," and the present loses its hold upon us, and the objects of sense wax faint and dim, there is often a strangely vivid light shed over our whole moral history. Our life rises before us in its complete development, and with the scars and wounds of sin just where we made them. The sorrow of an irreparable past comes upon us, and we are tortured in vain by the thought of the good we have thrown away, or of the evil we have made our portion.

Let no young man imagine for a moment that it can ever be unimportant whether he yields to this or that sinful passion, or, as it may appear to him at the time, venial indulgence. Let him not try to quiet his conscience by the thought that at the worst he will outlive the memory of his folly, and attain to a higher life in the future. Many may seem to him to have done this. Many of the greatest men have been, he may think, wild in youth. They have "sown their wild oats," as the saying is, and had done with them; and their future lives have only appeared the more remarkable in the view of the follies of their youth. A more mischievous delusion could not possibly possess the mind of any young man. For as surely as the innermost law of the world is the law of moral retribution, they who sow wild oats will reap, in some shape or another, a sour and bitter harvest. For "whatsoever a man soweth that shall he also reap; he that soweth to the flesh, shall of the flesh reap corruption; he that soweth to the Spirit, shall of the Spirit reap life everlasting."

There is nothing more sure than this law of moral connexion and retribution. Life, through all its course, is a series of moral impulses and consequences, each part of which bears the impress of all that goes before, and again communicates its impress to all that follows. And it is with the character, which is the sum of all, that we meet death, and enter on the life to come. Every act of life—all our work, and study, and enjoyment—our temptations, our sins, our repentance, our faith, our virtue are preparing us—whether we think it or not—for happiness or misery hereafter. It is this more than anything that gives such a solemn character to the occupations of life. They are the lessons for a higher life. They are an education—a discipline for hereafter. This is their highest meaning.

Let young men remember the essential bearing of the present upon the future. In beginning life let them remember the end of it, and how it will be at the end as it has been throughout. All will be summed up to this point; and the future and the eternal will take their character from the present and the temporary. " He that is unjust, let him be 'unjust still : and he which is filthy, let him be filthy still : and he that is righteous, let him be righteous still : and he that is holy, let him be holy still." The threads of our moral history run on in unbroken continuity. The shadow of death may cover them from the sight ; but they emerge in the world beyond in like order as they were here.

Make your present life, therefore, a preparation for death and the life to come.   Make it such by embracing now the light and love of God your Father—by doing the work of Christ your Saviour and Master— by using the world without abusing it—by seeking in all your duties, studies, and enjoyments, to become meet for a "better country, that is, an heavenly."   To the youngest among you the time may be short.   The summons to depart may come in "a day and an hour when you think not."   Happy then the young man whose Lord shall find him waiting—working—looking even from the portals of an opening life here to the gates of that celestial inheritance "incorruptible and undefiled, and that fadeth not away!"—*Tulloch.*

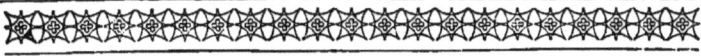

# THRIFT.

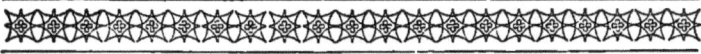

# THRIFT.

## INDUSTRY.

"Not what I have, but what I do, is my kingdom." — *Carlyle*.

" Productive industry is the only capital which enriches a people, and spreads national prosperity and well-being. In all labor there is profit, says Solomon. What is the science of Political Economy, but a dull sermon on this text? " — *Samuel Laing*.

" God provides the good things of the world to serve the needs of nature, by the labors of the ploughman, the skill and pains of the artizan, and the dangers and traffic of the merchant. . . . The idle person is like one that is dead, unconcerned in the changes and necessities of the world; and he only lives to spend his time, and eat the fruits of the earth: like a vermin or a wolf, when their time comes they die and perish, and in the meantime do no good." — *Jeremy Taylor*.

> "For the structure that we raise,
>     Time is with materials filled;
> Our to-days and yesterdays
>     Are the blocks with which we build." — *Longfellow*.

HRIFT began with civilization. It began when men found it necessary to provide for to-morrow, as well as for to-day. It began long before money was invented.

Thrift means private economy. It includes domestic economy, as well as the order and management of a family.

While it is the object of Private Economy to create and promote the well-being of individuals, it is the ob ject of Political Economy to create and increase the wealth of nations.

Private and public wealth have the same origin. Wealth is obtained by labor; it is preserved by savings and accumulations; and it is increased by diligence and perseverance.

It is the savings of individuals which compose the wealth — in other words, the well-being — of every nation.   On the other hand, it is the wastefulness of individuals which occasions the impoverishment of states.   So that every thrifty person may be regarded as a public benefactor, and every thriftless person as a public enemy.

There is no dispute as to the necessity for Private Economy.   Everybody admits it, and recommends it. But with respect to Political Economy, there are numerous discussions, — for instance, as to the distribution of capital, the accumulations of property, the incidence of taxation, the Poor Laws, and other subjects, — into which we do not propose to enter.   The subject of Private Economy, of Thrift, is quite sufficient by itself to occupy the pages of this book.

Economy is not a natural instinct, but the growth of experience, example, and forethought.   It is also the result of education and intelligence.   It is only when men become wise and thoughtful that they become frugal. Hence the best means of making men and women provident is to make them wise.

Prodigality is much more natural to man than thrift, The savage is the greatest of spendthrifts, for he has no forethought, no to-morrow. The prehistoric man saved nothing. He lived in caves, or in hollows of the ground covered with branches. He subsisted on shell-fish which he picked up on the seashore, or upon nuts which he gathered in the woods. He killed animals with stones. He lay in wait for them, or ran them down on foot. Then he learnt to use stones as tools ; making stone arrow-heads and spear-points, thereby utilizing his labor, and killing birds and animals more quickly.

The original savage knew nothing of agriculture. It was only in comparatively recent times that men gathered seeds for food, and saved a portion of them for next year's crop. When minerals were discovered, and fire was applied to them, and the minerals were smelted into metal, man made an immense stride. He could then fabricate hard tools, chisel stone, build houses, and proceed by unwearying industry to devise the manifold means and agencies of civilization.

The dweller by the ocean burnt a hollow in a felled tree, launched it, went to sea in it, and fished for food. The hollowed tree became a boat, held together with

iron nails. The boat became a galley, a ship, a paddle-
boat, a screw steamer, and the world was opened up for
colonization and civilization.

Man would have continued uncivilized, but for the
results of the useful labors of those who preceded him.
The soil was reclaimed by his predecessors, and made
to grow food for human uses. They invented tools and
fabrics, and we reap the useful results. They discovered art and science, and we succeed to the useful effects of their labors.

All nature teaches that no good thing which has once
been done passes utterly away. The living are ever
reminded of the buried millions who have worked and
won before them. The handicraft and skill displayed
in the buildings and sculptors of the long-lost cities of
Nineveh, Babylon, and Troy, have descended to the
present time. In nature's economy, no human labor is
altogether lost. Some remnant of useful effect continues to reward the race, if not the individual.

The mere material wealth bequeathed to us by our
forefathers forms but an insignificant item in the sum
of our inheritance. Our birthright is made up of something far more imperishable. It consists of the sum of
the useful effects of human skill and labor. These effects were not transmitted by learning, but by teaching
and example. One generation taught another, and thus

art and handicraft, the knowledge of mechanical appliances and materials, continued to be preserved. The labors and efforts of former generations were thus transmitted by father to son ; and they continue to form the natural heritage of the human race — one of the most important instruments of civilization.

Our birthright, therefore, consists in the useful effects of the labors of our forefathers ; but we cannot enjoy them unless we ourselves take part in the work. All must labor, either with hand or head. . Without work, life is worthless ; it becomes a mere state of moral coma. We do not mean merely physical work. There is a great deal of higher work — the work of action and endurance, of trial and patience, of enterprise and philanthropy, of spreading truth and civilization, of diminishing suffering and relieving the poor, of helping the weak, and enabling them to help themselves.

" A noble heart," says Barrow, " will disdain to subsist, like a drone, upon others' labors ; like a vermin to filch its food out of the public granary ; or, like a shark, to prey upon the lesser fry ; but it will rather outdo his private obligations to other men's care and toil, by considerable service and beneficence to the public ; for there is no calling of any sort, from the sceptre to the spade, the management whereof, with any good success, any credit, any satisfaction, doth not demand much work of the head, or of the hands, or of both."

Labor is not only a necessity, but it is also a pleasure. What would otherwise be a curse, by the constitution of our physical system becomes a blessing. Our life is a conflict with nature in some respects, but it is also a coöperation with nature in others. The sun, the air, and the earth are constantly abstracting from us our vital forces. Hence we eat and drink for nourishment, and clothe ourselves for warmth.

Nature works with us. She provides the earth which we furrow ; she grows and ripens the seeds that we sow and gather. She furnishes, with the help of human labor, the wool that we spin and the food that we eat. And it ought never to be forgotten, that however rich or poor we may be, all that we eat, all that we are clothed with, all that shelters us, from the palace to the cottage, is the result of labor.

Men coöperate with each other for the mutual sustenance of all. The husbandman tills the ground and provides food ; the manufacturer weaves tissues, which the tailor and seamstress make into clothes ; the mason and the bricklayer build the houses in which we enjoy household life. Numbers of workmen thus contribute and help to create the general result.

Labor and skill applied to the vulgarest things invest them at once with precious value. Labor is indeed the life of humanity ; take it away, banish it, and the race

11

of Adam were at once stricken with death. " He that will not work," said St. Paul, " neither shall he eat ; " and the apostle glorified himself in that he had labored with his own hands, and had not been chargeable to any man.

There is a well-known story of an old farmer calling his three idle sons around him when on his death-bed, to impart to them an important secret. " My sons," said he, " a great treasure lies hid in the estate which I am about to leave to you." The old man gasped. " Where is it hid ? " exclaimed the sons in a breath. " I am about to tell you," said the old man ; " you will have to dig for it ——" but his breath failed him before he could impart the weighty secret ; and he died. Forthwith the sons set to work with spade and mattock upon the long neglected fields, and they turned up every sod and clod upon the estate. They discovered no treasure, but they learnt to work ; and when the fields were sown, and the harvests came, lo ! the yield was prodigious, in consequence of the thorough tillage which they had undergone. Then it was that they discovered the treasure concealed in the estate, of which their wise old father had advised them.

Labor is at once a burden, a chastisement, an honor, and a pleasure. It may be identified with poverty, but there is also glory in it. It bears witness, at the same time, to our natural wants and to our manifold needs. What were man, what were life, what were civilization, without labor? All that is great in man comes of labor; — greatness in art, in literature, in science. Knowledge — " the wing wherewith we fly to heaven " — is only acquired through labor. Genius is but a capability of laboring intensely: it is the power of making great and sustained efforts. Labor may be a chastisement, but it is indeed a glorious one. It is worship, duty, praise, and immortality, — for those who labor with the highest aims, and for the purest purposes.

There are many who murmur and complain at the law of labor under which we live, without reflecting that obedience to it is not only in conformity with the Divine will, but also necessary for the development of intelligence, and for the thorough enjoyment of our common nature. Of all wretched men, surely the idle are the most so; — those whose life is barren of utility, who have nothing to do except to gratify their senses. Are not such men the most querulous, miserable, and dissatisfied of all, constantly in a state of *ennui*, alike useless to themselves and to others — mere cumberers of the earth, who when removed are missed by none, and whom none regret? Most wretched and ignoble lot, indeed, is the lot of the idlers.

Who have helped the world onward so much as the

workers; men who have had to work for necessity or from choice? All that we call progress — civilization, well-being, and prosperity — depends upon industry, diligently applied, — from the culture of a barley-stalk to the construction of a steamship, — from the stitching of a collar to the sculpturing of " the statue that enchants the world."

All useful and beautiful thoughts, in like manner, are the issue of labor, of study, of observation, of research, of diligent elaboration. The noblest poem cannot be elaborated, and send down its undying strains into the future, without steady and painstaking labor. No great work has ever been done " at a heat." It is the result of repeated efforts, and often of many failures. One generation begins, and another continues — the present coöperating with the past. Thus, the Parthenon began with a mud-hut; the Last Judgment with a few scratches on the sand. It is the same with individuals of the race; they begin with abortive efforts, which, by means of perseverance, lead to successful issues.

The history of industry is uniform in the character of its illustrations. Industry enables the poorest man to achieve honor, if not distinction. The greatest names in the history of art, literature, and science, are those of laboring men. A working instrument-maker gave us the steam-engine ; a barber, the spinning-machine ; a weaver, the mule ; a pitman perfected the locomotive ; — and working men of all grades have, one after another, added to the triumphs of mechanical skill.

By the working man, we do not mean merely the man who labors with his muscles and sinews. A horse can do this. But *he* is preëminently the working man who works with his brain also, and whose whole physical system is under the influence of his higher faculties. The man who paints a picture, who writes a book, who makes a law, who creates a poem, is a working man of the highest order, — not so necessary to the physical sustainment of the community as the ploughman or the shepherd ; but not less important as providing for society its highest intellectual nourishment.

Having said so much of the importance and the necessity of industry, let us see what uses are made of the advantages derivable from it. It is clear that man would have continued uncivilized but for the accumulations of savings made by his forefathers, — the savings of skill, of art, of invention, and of intellectual culture.

It is the savings of the world that have made the civilization of the world. Savings are the result of labor ; and it is only when laborers begin to save, that the results of civilization accumulate. We have said that thrift began with civilization : we might almost have said that thrift produced civilization. Thrift produces capital ; and capital is the conserved result of labor. The capitalist is merely a man who does not spend all that is earned by work.

But thrift is not a natural instinct. It is an acquired principle of conduct. It involves self-denial — the denial of present enjoyment for future good — the subordination of animal appetite to reason, forethought, and prudence. It works for to-day, but also provides for to-morrow. It invests the capital it has saved, and makes provision for the future.

" Man's right of seeing the future," says Mr. Edward Denison, " which is conferred on him by reason, has attached to it the duty of providing for that future ; and our language bears witness to this truth by using, as expressive of active precaution against future want, a word which in its radical meaning implies only a passive foreknowledge of the same. Whenever we speak of the *virtue of providence*, we assume that forewarned is fore-armed. To know the future is no virtue, but it is the greatest of virtues to prepare for it." [1]

But a large proportion of men do not provide for the

---

[1] *Letters of the late Edward Denison.*

future. They do not remember the past. They think only of the present. They preserve nothing. They spend all that they earn. They do not provide for themselves : they do not provide for their families. They may make high wages, but eat and drink the whole of what they earn. Such people are constantly poor, and hanging on the verge of destitution.

It is the same with nations. The nations which consume all that they produce, without leaving a store for future production, have no capital. Like thriftless individuals, they live from hand to mouth, and are always poor and miserable. Nations that have no capital, have no commerce. They have no accumulations to dispose of ; hence they have no ships, no sailors, no docks, no harbors, no canals, and no railways. Thrifty industry lies at the root of the civilization of the world.

Look at Spain. There, the richest soil is the least productive. Along the banks of the Guadalquivir, where once twelve thousand villages existed, there are now not eight hundred ; and they are full of beggars. A Spanish proverb says, " El cielo y suelo es bueno, el entresuelo malo " — The sky is good, the earth is good ; that only is bad which lies between the sky and the earth. Continuous effort, or patient labor, is for the Spaniard an insupportable thing. Half through indolence, half through pride, he cannot bend to work.

A Spaniard will blush to work ; he will not blush to beg ! [1]

It is in this way that society mainly consists of two classes — the savers and the wasters, the provident and the improvident, the thrifty and the thriftless, the Haves and the Have-nots.

The men who economize by means of labor become the owners of capital which sets other labor in motion. Capital accumulates in their hands, and they employ other laborers to work for them.    Thus trade and commerce begin.

The thrifty build houses, warehouses, and mills. They fit manufactories with tools and machines.    They build ships, and send them to various parts of the world.    They put their capital together, and build railroads, harbors, and docks.    They open up mines of coal, iron, and copper ; and erect pumping engines to keep them clear of water.    They employ laborers to work the mines, and thus give rise to an immense amount of employment.

All this is the result of thrift.    It is the result of economizing money, and employing it for beneficial purposes.    The thriftless man has no share in the progress of the world.    He spends all that he gets, and can give no help to anybody.    No matter how

[1] EUGENE POITOU — *Spain and its People.*

much money he makes, his position is not in any respect raised. He husbands none of his resources. He is always calling for help. He is, in fact, the born thrall and slave of the thrifty.

### HABITS OF THRIFT.

"Die Hauptsache ist dass man lerne sich selbst zu beherrschen." [The great matter is to learn to rule one's self.] — *Goethe.*

"Most men work for the present, a few for the future. The wise work for both — for the future in the present, and for the present in the future." — *Guesses at Truth.*

"The secret of all success is to know how to deny yourself. . . . If you once learn to get the whip-hand of yourself, that is the best educator. Prove to me that you can control yourself, and I'll say you're an educated man; and without this, all other education is good for next to nothing." — *Mrs. Oliphant.*

"All the world cries, 'Where is the man who will save us? We want a man! Don't look so far for this man. You have him at hand. This man — it is you, it is I, it is each one of us! . . . How to constitute one's self a man? Nothing harder, if one knows not how to *will* it; nothing easier, if one wills it." — *Alexandre Dumas.*

COMPETENCE and comfort lie within the reach of most people, were they to take the adequate means to secure and enjoy them. Men who are paid good wages might also become capitalists, and take their fair share in the improvement and well-being of the world. But it is only by the exercise of labor, energy, honesty, and thrift, that they can advance their own position or that of their class.

Society at present suffers far more from waste of money than from want of money. It is easier to make money than to know how to spend it. It is not what a man gets that constitutes his wealth, but his manner of spending and economizing. And when a man obtains by his labor more than enough for his personal and family wants, and can lay by a little store of savings besides, he unquestionably possesses the elements of social well-being. The savings may amount to little, but they may be sufficient to make him independent.

There is no reason why the highly-paid workman of to-day may not save a store of capital. It is merely a matter of self-denial and private economy. Indeed, the principal industrial leaders of to-day consist, for the most part, of men who have sprung directly from the ranks. It is the accumulation of experience and skill that makes the difference between the workman and the *no*-workman; and it depends upon the workman himself whether he will save his capital or waste it. If he save it, he will always find that he has sufficient opportunities for employing it profitably and usefully.

Thrift of Time is equal to thrift of money. Franklin said, "Time is gold." If one wishes to earn money, it may be done by the proper use of time. But time may also be spent in doing many good and noble actions. It may be spent in learning, in study, in art, in science, in literature. Time can be economized by system. System is an arrangement to secure certain ends, so that no time may be lost in accomplishing them. Every business man must be systematic and orderly. So must every housewife. There must be a place for everything, and everything in its place. There must also be a time for everything, and everything must be done in time.

It is not necessary to show that economy is useful. Nobody denies that thrift may be practised. We see numerous examples of it. What many men have already done, all other men *may* do. Nor is thrift a painful virtue. On the contrary, it enables us to avoid much contempt and many indignities. It requires us to deny ourselves, but not to abstain from any proper enjoyment. It provides many honest pleasures, of which thriftlessness and extravagance deprive us.

Thrift does not require superior courage, nor superior intellect, nor any superhuman virtue. It merely requires common sense, and the power of resisting selfish enjoyments. In fact, thrift is merely common sense in every-day working action. It needs no fervent resolution, but only a little patient self-denial. BEGIN is its device ! The more the habit of thrift is practised, the easier it becomes ; and the sooner it compensates the self-denier for the sacrifices which it has imposed.

The question may be asked, — Is it possible for a man working for small wages to save anything, and lay it by in a savings bank, when he requires every penny for the maintenance of his family? But the fact remains, that it *is* done by many industrious and sober men; that they do deny themselves, and put their spare earnings into savings banks, and the other receptacles provided for poor men's savings. And if some can do this, all may do it under similar circumstances, — without depriving themselves of any genuine pleasure, or any real enjoyment.

How intensely selfish it is for a person in the receipt of good pay to spend everything upon himself, — or, if he has a family, to spend his whole earnings from week to week, and lay nothing by. When we hear that a man, who has been in the receipt of a good salary, has died and left nothing behind him — that he has left his wife and family destitute — left them to chance — to live or perish anywhere, — we cannot but regard it as the most selfish thriftlessness. And yet, comparatively little is thought of such cases. Perhaps the hat goes round. Subscriptions may produce something — perhaps nothing; and the ruined remnants of the unhappy family sink into poverty and destitution.

Yet the merest prudence would, to a great extent, have obviated this result. The curtailment of any sensual and selfish enjoyment — of a glass of beer or a plug of tobacco — would enable a man, in the course of years, to save at least something for others, instead of wasting it on himself. It is, in fact, the absolute duty of the poorest man to provide, in however slight a degree, for the support of himself and his family in the season of sickness and helplessness which often comes upon men when they least expect such a visitation.

Comparatively few people can be rich ; but most have it in their power to acquire, by industry and economy, sufficient to meet their personal wants. They may even become the possessors of savings sufficient to secure them against penury and poverty in their old age. It is not, however, the want of opportunity, but the want of will that stands in the way of economy. Men may labor unceasingly with hand or head; but they cannot abstain from spending too freely, and living too highly.

The majority prefer the enjoyment of pleasure to the practice of self-denial. With the mass of men, the animal is paramount. They often spend all that they earn. But it is not merely the working people who are spendthrifts. We hear of men who for years have been earning and spending hundreds and thousands a year, who suddenly die, — leaving their children penniless. Everybody knows of such cases. At their death, the very furniture of the house they have lived in belongs to others. It is sold to pay their funeral expenses and the debts which they have incurred during their thriftless lifetime.

Money represents a multitude of objects without value, or without real utility ; but it also represents something much more precious,— and that is independence. In this light it is of great moral importance.

As a guarantee of independence, the modest and plebeian quality of economy is at once ennobled and raised to the rank of one of the most meritorious of virtues. " Never treat money affairs with levity," said Bulwer ; " Money is Character." Some of man's best qualities depend upon the right use of money, — such as his generosity, benevolence, justice, honesty, and forethought. Many of his worst qualities also originate in the bad use of money, — such as greed, miserliness, injustice, extravagance, and improvidence.

No class ever accomplished anything that lived from hand to mouth. People who spend all that they earn, are ever hanging on the brink of destitution. They must necessarily be weak and impotent — the slaves of time and circumstance. They keep themselves poor. They lose self-respect, as well as the respect of others. It is impossible that they can be free and independent. To be thriftless is enough to deprive one of all manly spirit and virtue.

But a man with something saved, no matter how

little, is in a different position.  The little capital he
has stored up is always a source of power.  He is no
longer the sport of time and fate.  He can boldly look
the world in the face.  He is, in a manner, his own
master.  He can dictate his own terms.  He can
neither be bought nor sold.  He can look forward with
cheerfulness to an old age of comfort and happiness.

As men become wise and thoughtful, they generally
become provident and frugal.  A thoughtless man,
like a savage, spends as he gets, thinking nothing of
to-morrow, of the time of adversity, or of the claims
of those whom he has made dependent on him.  But a
wise man thinks of the future ; he prepares in good
time for the evil day that may come upon him and his
family ; and he provides carefully for those who are
near and dear to him.

What a serious responsibility does the man incur
who marries !  Not many seriously think of this responsibility.  Perhaps this is wisely ordered.  For,
much serious thinking might end in the avoidance of
married life and its responsibilities.  But, once married, a man ought forthwith to determine that, so far
as his own efforts are concerned, want shall never enter
his household ; and that his children shall not, in the
event of his being removed from the scene of life and
labor, be left a burden upon society.

Economy with this object is an important duty. Without economy, no man can be just — no man can be honest. Improvidence is cruelty to women and children ; though the cruelty is born of ignorance. A father spends his surplus means in drink, providing little, and saving nothing ; and then he dies, leaving his destitute family his lifelong victims. Can any form of cruelty surpass this ? Yet this reckless course is pursued to a large extent among every class. The middle and upper classes are equally guilty with the lower class. They live beyond their means. They live extravagantly. They are ambitious of glare and glitter — frivolity and pleasure. They struggle to be rich, that they may have the means of spending, — of drinking rich wines, and giving good dinners.

When Mr. Hume said in the House of Commons, some years ago, that the tone of living in England was altogether too high, his observation was followed with "loud laughter." Yet his remark was perfectly true. It is far more true now than it was then. Thinking people believe that life is now too fast, and that we are living at high-pressure. In short, we live extravagantly. We live beyond our means. We throw away our earnings, and often throw our lives after them.

Many persons are diligent enough in making money, but do not know how to economize it, — or how to spend it. They have sufficient skill and industry to do the one, but they want the necessary wisdom to do the other. The temporary passion for enjoyment seizes us, and we give way to it without regard to consequences. And yet it may be merely the result of forgetfulness, and might be easily controlled by firmness of will, and by energetic resolution to avoid the occasional causes of expenditure for the future.

The habit of saving arises, for the most part, in the desire to ameliorate our social condition, as well as to ameliorate the condition of those who are dependent upon us. It dispenses with everything which is not essential, and avoids all methods of living that are wasteful and extravagant. A purchase made at the lowest price will be dear, if it be a superfluity. Little expenses lead to great. Buying things that are not wanted soon accustoms us to prodigality in other respects.

Cicero said, "Not to have a mania for buying, is to possess a revenue." Many are carried away by the habit of bargain-buying. "Here is something wonderfully cheap: let us buy it." "Have you any use for it?" "No, not at present; but it is sure to come in useful, some time." Fashion runs in this habit of buying. Some buy old china — as much as will furnish a china-shop. Others buy old pictures — old furniture —

12

all great bargains! There would be little harm in
buying these old things, if they were not so often
bought at the expense of the connoisseur's creditors.
Horace Walpole once said, " I hope that there will
not be another sale, for I have not an inch of room
nor a farthing left."

Men must prepare in youth and in middle age the
means of enjoying old age pleasantly and happily.
There can be nothing more distressing than to see an
old man who has spent the greater part of his life in
well-paid-for labor, reduced to the necessity of begging
for bread, and relying entirely on the commiseration of
his neighbors, or upon the bounty of strangers.   Such
a consideration as this should inspire men in early life
with a determination to work and to save, for the benefit of themselves and their families in later years.

It is, in fact, in youth that economy should be practised, and in old age that men should dispense liberally, provided they do not exceed their income.   The
young man has a long future before him, during which
he may exercise the principles of economy ; whilst the
other is reaching the end of his career, and can carry
nothing out of the world with him.

This, however, is not the usual practice.   The young
man now spends, or desires to spend, quite as liberally,
and often much more liberally, than his father, who

is about to end his career. He begins life where his father left off. He spends more than his father did at his age, and soon finds himself up to his ears in debt. To satisfy his incessant wants, he resorts to unscrupulous means, and to illicit gains. He tries to make money rapidly ; he speculates, over-trades, and is speedily wound up. Thus he obtains experience ; but it is the result, not of well-doing, but of ill-doing.

Socrates recommends fathers of families to observe the practice of their thrifty neighbors — of those who spend their means to the best advantage, — and to profit by their example. Thrift is essentially practical, and can best be taught by facts. Two men earn, say, two dollars a day. They are in precisely the same condition as respects family living, and expenditure. Yet the one says he cannot save, and does not ; while the other says he can save, and regularly deposits part of his savings in a savings bank, and eventually becomes a capitalist.

Samuel Johnson fully knew the straits of poverty. He once signed his name *Impransus*, or *Dinnerless*. He had walked the streets with Savage, not knowing where to lay his head at night. Johnson never forgot the poverty through which he passed in his early life, and he was always counselling his friends and readers to avoid it. Like Cicero, he averred that the best

source of wealth or well-being was economy. He called
it the daughter of Prudence, the sister of Temperance,
and the mother of Liberty.

"Poverty," he said, "takes away so many means of
doing good, and produces so much inability to resist
evil, both natural and moral, that it is by all virtuous
means to be avoided. Resolve, then, not to be poor;
whatever you have, spend less. Frugality is not only
the basis of quiet, but of beneficence. No man can
help others who wants help himself; we must have
enough before we have to spare."

And again he said, "Poverty is a great enemy to
human happiness. It certainly destroys liberty, and
it makes some virtues impracticable, and others extremely difficult. . . . All to whom want is terrible,
upon whatever principle, ought to think themselves
obliged to learn the sage maxims of our parsimonious
ancestors, and attain the salutary arts of contracting
expense; for without economy none can be rich, and
with it few can be poor."

When economy is looked upon as a thing that *must*
be practised, it will never be felt as a burden; and
those who have not before observed it, will be astonished to find what a few dimes or quarters laid
aside weekly, will do towards securing moral elevation,
mental culture, and personal independence.

There is a dignity in every attempt to economize. Its very practice is improving. It indicates self-denial, and imparts strength to the character. It produces a well-regulated mind. It fosters temperance. It is based on forethought. It makes prudence the dominating characteristic. It gives virtue the mastery over self-indulgence. Above all, it secures comfort, drives away care, and dispels many vexations and anxieties which might otherwise prey upon us.

Some will say, " It can't be done." But everybody can do something. " It can't " is the ruin of men and of nations. In fact, there is no greater cant that *can't*. Take an instance. A ten-cent cigar a day is equal to $36.50 a year. This sum will insure a man's life for $2,000, payable at death. The man who spends twenty cents a day, uselessly squanders in fifty years nearly ten thousand dollars.

A master recommended one of his workmen to " lay by something for a rainy day." Shortly after, the master asked the man how much he had added to his store. " Faith, nothing at all," said he ; " I did as you bid me ; but it rained very hard yesterday, and it all went — in drink ! "

That a man should maintain himself and his family without the help of others, is due to his sense of self-respect. Every genuine, self-helping man ought to

respect himself. He is the centre of his own little
world. His personal loves, likings, experiences, hopes,
and fears, — how important they are to him, although
of little consequence to others. They affect his happiness, his daily life, and his whole being as a man.
He cannot therefore but feel interested, deeply interested in all that concerns himself.

To do justice, a man must think well not only of
himself, but of the duties which he owes to others.
He must not aim too low, but regard man as created
"a little lower than the angels." Let him think of
his high destiny — of the eternal interests in which he
has a part — of the great scheme of nature and providence — of the intellect with which he has been endowed — of the power of loving conferred upon him —
of the home on earth provided for him ; and he will
cease to think meanly of himself. The poorest human
being is the centre of two eternities — the Creator
o'ershadowing all.

Hence, let every man respect himself, — his body,
his mind, his character. Self-respect, originating in
self-love, instigates the first step of improvement. It
stimulates a man to rise, to look upward, to develop
his intelligence, to improve his condition. Self-respect
is the root of most of the virtues — of cleanliness,
chastity, reverence, honesty, sobriety. To think

meanly of one's self is to sink; sometimes to descend a precipice at the bottom of which is infamy.

Every man can help himself to some extent. We are not mere straws thrown upon the current to mark its course; but possessed of freedom of action, endowed with power to stem the waves and rise above them, each marking out a course for himself. We can each elevate ourselves in the scale of moral being. We can cherish pure thoughts. We can perform good actions. We can live soberly and frugally. We can provide against the evil day. We can read good books, listen to wise teachers, and place ourselves under the divinest influences on earth. We can live for the highest purposes, and with the highest aims in view.

"Self-love and social are the same," says one of our poets. The man who improves himself, improves the world. He adds one more true man to the mass. And the mass being made up of individuals, it is clear that were each to improve himself, the result would be the improvement of the whole. Social advancement is the consequence of individual advancement. The whole cannot be pure, unless the individuals composing it are pure. Society at large is but the reflex of individual conditions. All this is but the repetition of a truism, but truisms have often to be repeated to make their full impression.

The sum and substance of our remarks is this : In all the individual reforms or improvements that we desire, we must begin with ourselves. We must exhibit our gospel in our own life. We must teach by our own example. If we would have others elevated, we must elevate ourselves. Each man can exhibit the results in his own person. He can begin with self-respect.

The uncertainty of life is a strong inducement to provide against the evil day. To do this is a moral and social, as well as a religious duty. "He that provideth not for his own, and especially for those of his own household, hath denied the faith, and is worse than an infidel."

The uncertainty of life is proverbially true. The strongest and healthiest man may be stricken down in a moment, by accident or disease. If we take human life in the mass, we cannot fail to recognize the uncertainty of life as much as we do the certainty of death.

There is a striking passage in Addison's "Vision of Mirza," in which life is pictured as a passage over a bridge of about a hundred arches. A black cloud hangs over each end of the bridge. At the entrance to it there are hidden pitfalls very thickly set, through which throngs disappear, so soon as they have placed

their feet upon the bridge. They grow thinner towards the centre; they gradually disappear; until at
length only a few persons reach the further side, and
these also having dropped through the pitfalls, the
bridge at its further extremity becomes entirely clear.
The description of Addison corresponds with the results of the observations made as to the duration of
human life.

Thus, of a hundred thousand persons born in this
country, it has been ascertained that a fourth of them
die before they have reached their fifth year; and one-
half before they have reached their fiftieth year. One
thousand one hundred will reach their ninetieth year.
Sixteen will live to a hundred. And only two persons
out of the hundred thousand — like the last barks of
an innumerable convoy, will reach the advanced and
helpless age of a hundred and five years.

Two things are very obvious, — the uncertainty as to
the hour of death in individuals, but the regularity and
constancy of the circumstances which influence the
duration of human life in the aggregate. It is a matter of certainty that the *average* life of all persons born
in this country extends to about forty-five years. This
has been proved by a very large number of observations of human life and its duration.

Equally extensive observations have been made as

to the average number of persons of various ages who die yearly. It is always the number of the experiments which gives the law of the probability. It is on such observations that the actuary founds his estimates of the mortality that exists at any given period of life. The actuary tells you that he has been guided by the Laws of Mortality. Now the results must be very regular, to justify the actuary in speaking of Mortality as governed by Laws. And yet it is so.

Indeed, there would seem to be no such thing as chance in the world. Man lives and dies in conformity to a law. A sparrow falls to the ground in obedience to a law. Nay, there are matters in the ordinary transactions of life, such as one might suppose were the mere result of chance, which are ascertained to be of remarkable accuracy when taken in the mass. For instance, the number of letters put in the post-office without an address; the number of letters wrongly directed; the number containing money; the number unstamped; continue nearly the same, in relation to the number of letters posted, from one year to another.

Now, it is the business of man to understand the laws of health, and to provide against their consequences, — as, for instance, in the matter of sickness, accident, and premature death. We cannot escape the consequences of transgression of the natural laws, though we may have meant well. We must have done well. The Creator does not alter His laws to accommodate them to our ignorance. He has furnished us with intelligence, so that we may understand them and act upon them : otherwise we must suffer the consequences in inevitable pain and sorrow.

We often hear the cry raised, "Will nobody help us?" It is a spiritless, hopeless cry. It is sometimes a cry of revolting meanness, especially when it issues from those who with a little self-denial, sobriety, and thrift, might easily help themselves.

Many people have yet to learn, that virtue, knowledge, freedom, and prosperity must spring from themselves. Legislation can do very little for them: it cannot make them sober, intelligent, and well-doing. The prime miseries of most men have their origin in causes far removed from acts of the legislature.

The spendthrift laughs at legislation. The drunkard defies it, and arrogates the right of dispensing with forethought and self-denial, — throwing upon others the blame of his ultimate wretchedness. The mob orators, who gather "the millions" about them, are very wide of the mark, when, instead of seeking to train their crowd of hearers to habits of frugality, temperance, and self-culture, they encourage them to keep up the cry, "Will nobody help us?"

The cry sickens the soul.  It shows gross ignorance of the first elements of personal welfare.  Help is in men themselves.  They were born to help and to elevate themselves.  They must work out their own salvation.  The poorest men have done it : why should not every man do it?  The brave, upward spirit ever conquers.

The number of well-paid workmen in this country has become very large, who might easily save and economize, to the improvement of their moral well-being, of their respectability and independence, and of their status in society as men and citizens.  They are improvident and thriftless to an extent which proves not less hurtful to their personal happiness and domestic comfort, than it is injurious to the society of which they form so important a part.

In " prosperous times " they spend their gains recklessly, and when adverse times come, they are at once plunged in misery.  Money is not used, but abused ; and when wage-earning people should be providing against old age, or for the wants of a growing family, they are, in too many cases, feeding folly, dissipation, and vice.  Let no one say that this is an exaggerated picture.  It is enough to look round in any neighborhood, and see how much is spent and how little is saved ; what a large proportion of earnings goes to the beershop, and how little to the savings bank or the benefit society.

"Prosperous times" are very often the least prosperous of all times. In prosperous times, mills are working full time ; men, women, and children are paid high wages ; warehouses are emptied and filed ; goods are manufactured and exported ; carts full of produce pass along the streets; immense freight trains run along the railways, and heavily-laden ships leave our shores daily for foreign ports, full of the products of our industry. Everybody seems to be becoming richer and more prosperous. But we do not think of whether men and women are becoming wiser, better trained, less self-indulgent, more religiously disposed, or living for any higher purpose than the satisfaction of the animal appetite.

If this apparent prosperity be closely examined, it will be found that expenditure is increasing in all directions. There are demands for higher wages ; and the higher wages, when obtained, are spent as soon as earned. Intemperate habits are formed, and, once formed, the habit of intemperance continues. Increased wages, instead of being saved, are for the most part spent.

Thus, when a population is thoughtless and improvident, no kind of material prosperity will benefit them.

Unless they exercise forethought and economy they will alternately be in a state of "hunger and burst." When trade falls off, as it usually does after exceptional prosperity, they will not be comforted by the thought of what they *might* have saved, had it ever occurred to them that the "prosperous times" might not prove permanent.

If man's chief end were to manufacture cloth, silk, cotton, hardware, toys, and china; to cultivate land, grow corn, and graze cattle; to live for mere money profit, and hoard or spend, as the case might be, we might then congratulate ourselves upon our National Prosperity.  But is this the chief end of man ?  Has he not faculties, affections, and sympathies, besides muscular organs ?  Has not his mind and heart certain claims, as well as his mouth and his back ?  Has he not a soul as well as a stomach ?  And ought not "prosperity" to include the improvement and well-being of his morals and intellect as well as of his bones and muscles ?

Mere money is no indication of prosperity.  A man's nature may remain the same.  It may even grow more stunted and deformed, while he is doubling his expenditure, or adding cent. per cent. to his hoards yearly. It is the same with the mass.  The increase of their gains may merely furnish them with increased means for gratifying animal indulgences, unless their moral character keeps pace with their physical advancement. Double the gains of an uneducated, overworked man, in a time of prosperity, and what is the result? Simply that you have furnished him with the means of eating and drinking more! Thus, not even the material well-being of the population is secured by that condition of things which is defined by political economists as " National Prosperity." And so long as the moral elements of the question are ignored, this kind of "prosperity" is, we believe, calculated to produce far more mischievous results than good. It is knowledge and virtue alone that can confer dignity on a man's life; and the growth of such qualities in a nation are the only true marks of its real prosperity; not the infinite manufacture and sale of cotton prints, toys, hardware, and crockery.

In making the preceding observations we do not in the least advocate the formation of miserly, penurious habits; for we hate the scrub, the miser. All that we contend for is, that man should provide for the future, — that they should provide during good times for the bad times which almost invariably follow them, — that they should lay by a store of savings as a break-water against want, and make sure of a little fund which may maintain them in old age, secure their self-respect, and add to their personal comfort and social

well-being.    Thrift is not in any way connected with
avarice, usury, greed, or selfishness.    It is, in fact, the
very reverse of these disgusting dispositions    It means
economy for the purpose of securing independence.
Thrift requires that money should be used and not
abused — that it should be honestly earned and eco-
nomically employed —

> " Not for to put it in a hedge,
> Not for a train attendant, —
> But for the glorious privilege
> Of being Independent."

### METHODS OF ECONOMY.

" It was with profound wisdom that the Romans called by the same name courage and virtue.    There is in fact no virtue, properly so called, without victory
over ourselves : and what costs us nothing, is worth nothing." — *De Maistre.*

" Almost all the advantages which man possesses above the inferior animals,
arise from his power of acting in combination with his fellows ; and of accomplishing by the united efforts of numbers what could not be accomplished by the
detached efforts of individuals." — *J. S. Mill.*

" For the future, our main security will be in the wider diffusion of Property,
and in all such measures as will facilitate this result.    With the possession of property will come Conservative instincts, and disinclination for rash and reckless
schemes. . . . We trust much, therefore, to the rural population becoming Pro-
prietors, and to the urban population becoming Capitalists." — *W. R. Greg.*

THE methods of practicing economy are very simple.
Spend less than you earn.    That is the first rule.    A
portion should always be set apart for the future.    The
person who spends more than he earns, is a fool.    The
civil law regards the spendthrift as akin to the lunatic,

and frequently takes from him the management of his
own affairs.

The next rule is to pay ready money, and never, on
any account, to run into debt.   The person who runs
into debt is apt to get cheated ; and if he runs into debt
to any extent, he will himself be apt to get dishonest.
" Who pays what he owes, enriches himself."

The next is, never to anticipate uncertain profits by
expending them before they are secured.   The profits
may never come, and in that case you will have taken
upon yourself a load of debt which you may never get
rid of.    It will sit upon your shoulders like the old
man in Sinbad.

Another method of economy is, to keep a regular account of all that you earn, and of all that you expend.
An orderly man will know beforehand what he requires,
and will be provided with the necessary means for obtaining it.    Thus his domestic budget will be balanced ;
and his expenditure kept within his income.

John Wesley regularly adopted this course.   Although he possessed a small income, he always kept
his eyes upon the state of his affairs.   A year before
his death, he wrote with a trembling hand, in his Journal of Expenses ; " For more than eighty-six years I
have kept my accounts exactly.   I do not care to continue to do so any longer, having the conviction that I

13

economize all that I obtain, and give all that I can, —
that is to say all that I have."

Besides these methods of economy, the eye of the
master or the mistress is always necessary to see that
nothing is lost, that everything is put to its proper use
and kept in its proper place, and that all things are
done decently and in order.   It does no dishonor to
even the highest individuals to take a personal interest
in their own affairs.   And with persons of moderate
means, the necessity for the eye of the master overlooking everything, is absolutely necessary for the
proper conduct of business.

It is difficult to fix the precise limits of economy.
Bacon says that if a man would live well within his income, he ought not to expend more than one-half and
save the rest.   This is perhaps too exacting ; and Bacon
himself did not follow his own advice.   What proportion of one's income should be expended on rent?
That depends upon circumstances.   It is at all events
better to save too much, than spend too much.   One
may remedy the first defect, but not so easily the latter.
Wherever there is a large family, the more money that
is put to one side and saved, the better.

Economy is necessary to the moderately rich, as well
as to the comparatively poor man.   Without economy,
a man cannot be generous.   He cannot take part in

the charitable work of the world. If he spends all that he earns, he can help nobody. He cannot properly educate his children, nor put them in the way of starting fairly in the business of life. Even the example of Bacon shows that the loftiest intelligence cannot neglect thrift without peril. But thousands of witnesses daily testify, that men even of the most moderate intelligence, can practise the virtue with success.

Although the American people are a diligent, hard-working, and generally self-reliant race, trusting to themselves and their own efforts for their sustenance and advancement in the world, they are yet liable to overlook and neglect some of the best practical methods of improving their position, and securing their social well-being. They are not yet sufficiently educated to be temperate, provident, and foreseeing. They live for the present, and are too regardless of the coming time. Men who are husbands and parents, generally think they do their duty if they provide for the hour that is, neglectful of the hour that is to come. Though industrious, they are improvident ; though money-making, they are spendthrift. They do not exercise forethought enough, and are defective in the virtue of prudent economy.

Men of all classes are, as yet, too little influenced by these considerations. They are apt to live beyond their incomes, — at all events, to live up to them. The upper classes live too much for display; they must keep up their "position in society;" they must have fine houses, horses, and carriages; give good dinners, and drink rich wines; their ladies must wear costly and gay dresses. Thus the march of improvidence goes on over broken hearts, ruined hopes, and wasted ambitions.

The vice descends in society, — the middle classes strive to ape the patrician orders; they flourish crests, liveries, and hammercloths; their daughters must learn "accomplishments" — see "society" — ride and drive — frequent operas and theatres. Display is the rage, ambition rivalling ambition; and thus the vicious folly rolls on like a tide. The vice again descends. The working classes, too, live up to their means — much smaller means, it is true; but even when they are able, they are not sufficiently careful to provide against the evil day; and then only the poorhouse offers its scanty aid to protect them against want.

# SELF-MADE MEN.

# SELF-MADE MEN.

THE biography of every man who has risen to eminence of any kind by his own talent and industry, is a lesson and stimulus to all who read it. Self-made men are living witnesses that God has endowed man with the material and powers necessary to accomplish the most desirable fortune and fame, and that it is by no means essential to a man's success or greatness that he has, or has not, the inherited appliances of aristocratic birth, wealth, and consequent position, "forearming him" for his encounter with the world.

The greatest names on the page of history belong to men who have risen from obscure birth, against wealth, and in defiance of what is called disadvantageous position. Bearing in their nature the sacred fire, they have kindled at the breath of the opposing tempest, and by unwearied, undaunted struggle, dawned day by day into a broader, stronger, and more beautiful life. Such men, trusting to no fortuitous aids, and owing nothing to chances, have so beaten their pathway upward that they could not be thrust down by the accidents which disarm and discourage the mere favorite of circumstances.

It is not the men who have inherited most, except it is in nobility of soul and purpose, who have risen highest; but rather the men with no dower save soul and purpose, who have made fortunate and adverse circumstances alike a spur to goad their steed up the steep and stubborn mount, where

" Fame's proud temple shines afar."

To such men, every possible goal is accomplishable, and honest ambition has no height which genius or talent may tread, which has not felt the impress of their feet.

The list of men who have risen from obscurity—and in some cases poverty—to fame and fortune, is a long one, and would occupy more space than can be given within the compass of a reasonable book.

From a farm to the Presidential chair seems a long distance, but Abraham Lincoln traveled that distance, became President of the United States, and left behind him a name and reputation which will never die. Andrew Johnson began life as a tailor, and subsequently rose to the position of chief officer of the nation. George Peabody, when a boy, was an apprentice in a country store, and ended as a millionaire, leaving behind him a reputation for philanthropy which will never be forgotten. John Jacob Astor began life as a fur beater, and amassed an immense fortune. A. T. Stewart, from a school teacher, became the owner of the largest dry-goods house in the country, and one of the wealthiest men in the world. Cyrus W. Field was in early life a clerk, and to him, in a great measure, the world is indebted for the successful completion of the Atlantic cable. Samuel F. B. Morse, from an artist, became the inventor of the electric telegraph. Elihu B. Washburne, when a boy, worked in a printing office, and has risen to a very high position in the government of the nation. Dwight L. Moody, the great evangelist, from an uneducated, humble city missionary in Chicago, has been the means of infusing new life and energy into the Christian church, both in Great Britain and America; and has preached before the most learned and educated men of the day. And the great and illustrious General, and twice President of America, Ulysses S. Grant, began life as a tanner. His career is a marvellous one, and his ability and patriotism have been generously recognized, not only by the American people,

but by the whole world.   Charles Dickens, the great
novelist, began life as a newspaper reporter, and his
name and fame are now world-wide.   Thomas Carlyle,
a farmer's son, stands to-day at the head of the literary
profession, and is known as "The Chelsea Philosopher."   His writings and utterances show him to be a
far-seeing, acute, and clear-headed observer, and his
fame is already honored by all classes of the people.

We append a few sketches of prominent men, who
have risen from the ranks, and whose lives form noble
examples of perseverance under difficulties, and of
triumph over all obstacles.

# ELIHU B. WASHBURNE.

IF it be true of men that "blood will tell," the success in life achieved by Elihu B. Washburne, of Illinois, who was a farmer's boy, a printer's apprentice, who has been a lawyer, statesman, and diplomat, and who is to-day foremost among the men who may claim to be representative Americans, is to a great extent accounted for in advance. His father, Israel Washburne, was a native of Massachusetts, a man of high honor and sterling integrity, who removed to the district of Maine in 1806, and in 1809 settled at Livermore, Oxford County, that State, where he died in September, 1876, at the age of 92 years. Mr. Washburne's mother was a daughter of Samuel Benjamin, who descended directly from the Pilgrim Fathers, and who figured prominently in the Revolutionary War.

Mr. Washburne was the third of seven brothers,

several of whom have held important positions in the country's service.

Springing from such stock, Elihu B. Washburne was born at Livermore, in Oxford County, in September, 1816. The simple story of his early youth, filled as it is with notes of many vicissitudes, and being as it was a constant struggle, a ceaseless battle to wring hard fare from inhospitable surroundings, is not only most interesting but exceedingly instructive. From his earliest infancy young Elihu was taught to believe that there was no nonsense in this life, and that the best men, unlike the *Vicar of Wakefield*, never tired of being always wise. His father kept a small country store, and he, as early as his 7th year, was taught to "make himself generally useful," gathering chips, carrying wood, picking stones from off the sterile pasture land, driving cows, and doing many other "chores" of the same sort. He went to school a few weeks in winter, and again for a few weeks in summer; but, as may readily be imagined, learned but little. About his father's store, however, being a lad of keenest intelligence, he picked up much useful and miscellaneous information.

In June, 1833, he secured the situation of an apprentice in the office of the *Christian Intelligencer*, published at Gardiner, Me., and in his new position learned rapidly. In addition to the rudiments of his trade, he picked up much odd information, and as politics ran high at the time, and the newspaper office was the great place for political discussion, he soon became thoroughly conversant with all the election news of the period. Taking his cue from his father, who once in his hearing had denounced Andrew Jackson as utterly unfit to be President, as an officer who had hanged men in Florida without warrant of law, who had trampled the rights of the Judiciary under foot at New Orleans—he even at this early age conceived a bitter dislike to the Democracy, which clung to him in all his after life, and did much to make him, as he since has been, one of the leaders of the Republican party. Of this period in his career, Mr. Washburne wrote, some years ago, in a private diary: " As time rolled on, I was quite pleased and contented in my trade. I learned to set type rapidly, and had also begun to work a little at the press. I did not consider that I had to labor very hard, and I had a good deal of leisure time to read and study. I read all the exchange papers, and contracted the habit of newspaper reading, which has not left me to this day. I don't think I ever wasted an hour, but devoted myself entirely to the acquisition of knowledge. To a boy who is desirous of educating himself, there is not a

II

better school than a printing-office. I am satisfied
that I learned more in the one year I was in the
*Intelligencer* office than I ever learned in any one
year of my life."

Unfortunately, the boy's pleasant situation was not
long to continue. The paper with which he was connected failed, and he was thrown out into the world
without employment or any hope of obtaining another
situation. Still he did not despair, and, returning to
the neighborhood of his home, by the influence of
friends, after passing a severe examination, he was
selected to teach the district school, his compensation
being $10 a month, and it being stipulated that he was
to "board around" among the neighboring families.
He was barely 18 years of age when he entered upon
the duties of schoolmaster. Many of his pupils were
much older and stronger than himself, several of them
were notorious mischief-makers, and the winter before
the schoolmaster had been, by a number of riotous
pupils, turned bodily out of the school and the school
itself closed up. By every means in his power, desiring to avoid a collision with them, the young master
tried to conciliate his scholars, and for a while succeeded admirably. After the second week, however,
he began to see symptoms of revolt, and he made up
his mind that upon the first opportunity he would give

the big boys who were disposed to be impertinent a taste of his mettle. He soon had the opportunity. The class was up before him for recitation, when one of the biggest and worst lads in school not only declined to obey his orders, but impertinently laughed in his face. Without a word young Washburne sprang from his place, and, with a heavy ruler, beat the rebellious pupil so vigorously over the head and shoulders that he soon cried for mercy, and, together with his companions who had been most unruly, ever afterward submitted to discipline meekly and without dispute. Schoolmaster Washburne had no further trouble in maintaining the decorum of the establishment.

When his three months' term as a school-teacher had closed, and he had received his $30, he succeeded, after much effort, in securing a place as apprentice in the office of the Kennebec *Journal*, at Augusta, Me., which was the leading Whig organ of the State.

Young Washburne, though working very hard, sometimes until 2 or 3 o'clock in the morning, when a tri-weekly paper was published during sessions of the Legislature, had what seemed to him to be a very pleasant and rather easy place in the Kennebec *Journal* office, and he was very hopeful of becoming most proficient in his trade, when he was stricken by an ailment which prevented him permanently from standing at the "case." This was a great blow, but notwithstanding the disappointment, and finding that one career was closed to him, he, with his usual energy, turned his attention to another. He decided to study law, and in the spring of 1836 bade farewell to Augusta and the Kennebec *Journal*, going with what little money he had scraped together to the Kent's Hill Seminary, where he intended to study as long as his funds would hold out.

In the winter of 1836–'37, he studied Latin and French, read continuously, attended lyceum lectures, and progressed rapidly. He entered the law office of the Hon. John Otis, a distinguished lawyer, and member of Congress, who lived in the aristocratic town of Hallowell, Me., and in time Mr. Otis was so much struck by his diligence, fidelity, and ambition, that he aided him pecuniarily, and took him into his own family to board. Afterward, when the young man was fitted, Mr. Otis advanced him the money to enter the Cambridge Law School. Before this, however, in January, 1838, the Whigs having a majority in the Legislature, young Washburne, urged by his friends, tried to procure the position of Assistant Clerk to the House, which paid $2 a day, and would literally have been a god-send to him. He was defeated in this aspiration, but afterward was given some writing to do by the Secretary of State—who subsequently became his colleague in Congress. In March, 1839, he entered the Cambridge Law School, which was then most popular, having for its professors Mr. Justice Story and Simon Greenleaf, two of the most distinguished jurists the country has ever produced. Many of those who studied with Mr. Washburne have since become noted men in the nation.

For more than a year the young man pursued his studies at Cambridge, and then, having passed a critical examination, and having been admitted to the Bar, he determined to cut loose from his old associations, seek a home in the far West, and make for himself a competence. Gathering together what money he could, and, equipped by a careful mother with a few articles of clothing, he set out on his journey for the " West," but with no definite idea of what point he would ultimately select for settlement.

On his way to the West he passed through Washington, and then, for the first time, being thrown into the society of many distinguished men, he was naturally much impressed. Years afterward, writing of that first visit, he says: " The Senate of the United States was then in the very zenith of its power. Looking to the great men who were then members of it, we may well say 'there were giants in those days.' Clay, Webster, Calhoun, Benton, Preston, Buchanan, McDuffie, Silas Wright, are the names of some of the Senators which occur to me after the lapse of nearly thirty-five years. I can distinctly call to mind the personal appearance of every one of those men."

Pleasant as was this visit to Washington, however, young Washburne was unable to prolong it.  He was soon reminded, by the rapid decrease in his small hoard of money, that it would be necessary for him to push on, and leaving Washington, he, by slow stages, over rough roads, and making long trips on river steamboats, at last, in the spring of 1840, landed at Galena, in Illinois, the State in which he was afterwards to become famous.

When Elihu B. Washburne arrived in Galena, as I have described, a young man in a strange place, without friends or money, and with nothing to aid him in the world except a sound English education, much hard experience, and a high resolve, no man would have been foolhardy enough to predict that he would, in the time to come, grow with the growth of his new home, and, keeping abreast with the progress of the Great West, make for himself a name known not only in the nation, but throughout much of the civilized world.  Galena, at the time in question, was a town of about 1,800 inhabitants, of great business activity, and the centre of a large mining country. The Bar of the town was one of the most distinguished in Illinois, and the young Eastern lawyer, commencing the practice of his profession among many keen-witted men, found that he must do his best if he would sustain himself. He arrived at Galena shortly after the commencement of the memorable Harrison campaign, and, being a strong Whig, he made numerous speeches in support of that party. In 1844 he was made a delegate to the Whig National Convention, which met at Baltimore, and which with unbounded enthusiasm nominated to the Presidency that prince of political leaders, Henry Clay. Indeed, he was always one of Clay's stanchest, most steadfast, and at the same time most disinterested admirers. After the Convention was over, he went to Washington to see and congratulate Mr. Clay upon his nomination. He had never seen him before, and was as much impressed with his tall and striking figure as he was by his wondrous graciousness and affability of manner.

During all this time, and while taking so active a part in politics, it must not be assumed that Mr. Washburne neglected his law business. Such was not the case. His practice increased rapidly, and he attended to it faithfully. He practiced not only in his

own neighborhood, but also in the Supreme Court at
Springfield, the State Capital, making the journey to
that place by stage-coach, the trip occupying often
four or five days. In 1848, however, he was brought
forward by his friends as a candidate for the nomination for Congress in the Galena district—a district,
by the way, which at that time extended from Galena
half way to St. Louis. The nominating convention
met at Rock Island, and in it Col. Baker carried off
the nomination.

Notwithstanding the defeat which he thus encountered, Mr. Washburne developed such strength in the
convention as to make him more than ever a prominent man in the district. In 1852 he was again delegate to the National Whig Convention, and strongly
advocated and aided in the nomination of Gen. Scott
as against the pro-slavery influences of the convention. Because of this, when the Galena district was
reapportioned in two years after, he was again prominently mentioned in connection with the Congressional nomination, and was nominated. Washburne
canvassed the district with untiring zeal, and, greatly
to the surprise of his opponents and the people of the
State, he was elected by a majority of 286 votes.

Going to Congress, and representing as he did, what
was believed to have been an overwhelmingly Demo-

cratic district, Mr. Washburne was careful to feel well
his ground before attempting to make any display.
He did not believe, as do many of the young members of to-day, that it was his duty, before he had
well warmed his seat, to make half a dozen speeches,
which had been prepared in advance, before a look-
ing-glass in a private room.  He watched carefully
what was being done by those around him, and, knowing well the French proverb, may have believed that
" everything is possible to the man who waits."  So
successful was he in the first Congress to which he was
elected, and so admirably did he represent not only a
party, but all the people of his district, that in 1854,
when it again became necessary to elect a Congressman, he was elected by a majority of over 5,000.  In
the next Congress, the first regular session of which
commenced in 1855, he was made chairman of the
Committee on Commerce.  In that position he distinguished himself by a fidelity to business, and a
broad comprehension of the duties of his office.  Two
years later he was re-elected to Congress for the third
successive term.  During the session of that Congress
there occurred the fight on the floor of the House
between Galusha A. Grow, of Pennsylvania, and the
South Carolina " fire-eater," Lawrence M. Keitt.  Keitt,
of South Carolina, struck Grow, of Pennsylvania,

as he was walking through the aisle of the House of Representatives. Both represented great States. The South Carolinian looked for an easy conquest. The South Carolinian was mistaken. Grow returned the blow. For a moment there was consternation in the House. Then other Southerners, true to their traditions, rushed to the aid of their champion. But Mr. Grow, to the surprise of the Southerners, was not left unprotected. Many Northern men, with strong Anglo-Saxon arms, rushed to his support. Foremost among them was Elihu B. Washburne, who, with sturdy strokes of a fist developed by hard toil upon a New England farm, struck right and left in the just cause, and did much to demonstrate upon proud Southern cheeks that Yankee mud-sills would fight.

This little episode did Mr. Washburne no harm. When the election again came around he was again chosen from the Galena district, by an increased majority. In 1860 he was re-elected for the fifth successive time by a majority of 13,511—the largest majority given to any man in that Congress, and one of the largest given to any man who ever sat in the United States House of Representatives.

In the next Congress, and in those which followed it—for Mr. Washburne was triumphantly re-elected term after term—he, as chairman of the Committee on

Commerce, and later, as chairman of the Committee on Appropriations, took a most prominent part. He was one of the first of the men who, with far-sighted intelligence, saw that the war was not to be for thirty days, but might be for years. He was also regarded as the next friend of President Lincoln. Indeed, it was his duty, on the part of the House, to go with Mr. Seward on the part of the Senate, to receive Abraham Lincoln when, after his election for the first time, he came to Washington.

Lincoln was inaugurated, it is true, without bloodshed, but soon afterward the war came on, and everything was very far from being "all right" in Washington. During all the terrible days which followed, during the long and weary years of rebellion which were precipitated on the country by the slave-holding power, Elihu B. Washburne was a foremost figure in the council-chamber of the nation. He was again and again re-elected to Congress, till at last, by reason of the length of his continuous service, he became the "Father of the House." In that capacity he swore in Schuyler Colfax as Speaker on three different occasions, and swore in Mr. Speaker Blaine once. In the passage of all the great war legislation of the time he took an active part. He was always in his place fighting "steals" of every kind with a persistency which was almost heroic, and by his determined opposition to jobs of all kinds, earned the name of the "Watch-dog of the Treasury."

Gen. Grant, being one of Mr. Washburne's constituents, owed much of his rank in the army to his influence. Indeed, every promotion which he received was given either solely or in part, upon the recommendation of Mr. Washburne. The manner in which he (Grant) became senior Brigadier-General of Illinois Volunteers is now for the first time narrated. When the State in question had raised thirty-six regiments of troops, and was entitled to nine Brigadier-Generals, President Lincoln sent to each of the Illinois .delegation, Senators and Congressmen, a personal note asking them to recommend nine men to fill the vacant positions. The delegation was called to meet in Judge Trumball's room, and, after some discussion as to the manner in which the selections should be made, it was decided that the districts should be called in their numerical order, that each Congressman should name his candidate, and that his associates should then vote for or against him. The Galena district was the first one called, and, in response, Mr. Washburne suggested Colonel Grant, of Galena. The Colonel was not unknown to the other members of the delegation, and for this reason, as much as a desire to gratify Mr. Washburne, every member of the delegation voted for him, and he was in this way unanimously recommended as the first choice of the State for one of the nine positions which the President desired to fill. By virtue of thus appearing at the head of the Brigadier-Generals, as it afterward turned out, Grant took senior rank, and when it became necessary to make Major-Generals by promotion, for the simple reason that his name was at the head of the list as described, he was the first to receive the higher rank. Later on Mr. Washburne was instrumental in framing and passing the bill which made U. S. Grant a Lieutenant-General and, subsequently, General of the Armies of the United States. The first postal-telegraph bill ever introduced in the House was introduced by Mr. Washburne, and the bill providing for the establishment of national cemeteries (which became a law) was also introduced by him.

There is reason to believe that Gen. Grant was always very grateful to Mr. Washburne for the good service which he did him when he was a comparatively obscure citizen, and afterward when he had made a name. At all events, in 1869, when he had been elected President, one of his first acts was to appoint Congressman Washburne to the first place in his Cabinet. The appointment was made in a manner

exceedingly characteristic of Gen. Grant. It is a fact
beyond dispute that, as in the case of Don Cameron,
Mr. Washburne was entirely ignoraat of the President's intention to make him one of his Secretaries.
The great Illinois Congressman, immediately after the
President's inauguration, was sitting in his room in the
Capitol—the room of the Committee on Appropriations, which he took possession of after the death of
Thad. Stevens—and was discussing with Horace
Greeley and two or three other gentlemen the prob-
able action of President Grant in regard to his Cabi
net. Even while they were talking, a page-boy came
in from the Senate Chamber, saying:

"Mr. Washburne, here are a number of important
Executive appointments."

Mr. Washburne took the paper which the lad handed
him, and, greatly to his surprise, read at the top of the
list :

"To be Secretary of State, Elihu B. Washburne, of
Illinois."

Turning to Mr. Greeley and the other gentlemen
who were present, he said :

"The question is at last settled, gentlemen, and,
strangely enough, to be Secretary of State, President
Grant has named myself."

It is worthy of repetition that Mr. Washburne was

in this way for the first time informed of his appointment. He had absolutely no previous information of President Grant's intention toward himself.

To enter the Cabinet, he reluctantly resigned his seat in Congress, and bade farewell to a constituency which for nearly twenty years had honored themselves by honoring him. I say that he resigned reluctantly. He did so not only because he was sorry to discontinue his Congressional services under the old pleasant auspices, but because his health would not permit him to perform the duties of the new position to which he had been called. Such proved to be the case. After a short term of service and consultation with eminent physicians, he was fully assured that the duties of the State Department were more than he could hope to fulfill with safety to himself, and he resigned.

Subsequently President Grant tendered Mr. Washburne the position of Minister to France, which he accepted.

When Mr. Washburne resigned his position as Secretary of State, and, because of ill-health and a desire for rest, took upon himself the duties of the Ministership to France, he reckoned very much without his host. Indeed, he had only been a few months abroad when he discovered that his new post was destined to prove a most laborious, if not a very dangerous one.

By his logical and forcible appeals, Mr. Washburne succeeded, practically upon his own terms, in effecting the release from confinement within the French limits, of nearly all the German subjects who desired to return to their own country. Writing to the American Secretary of State under date of Sept. 2, 1870, he thus modestly tells of the remarkable success he had in the direction indicated: " The greater part of the German population has left Paris. This Legation has vised passports and given safe conducts for very nearlɪ 30,000 persons, subjects of the North German Con federation, expelled from France. We have giveu railroad tickets to the Prussian frontier for 8,000 of these people, as well as small amounts of money to a much smaller number. From this statement you will form somewhat of an estimate of the amount of labor we have performed for the past few weeks. * * * My time is now a good deal taken up in looking after Germans who have been arrested and thrown into prison. The number is very great, but my applications are promptly attended to, and thus far every man has been released for whom I have applied."

During all these terrible days of the bloody siege of Paris, and reign of the Commune, Elihu B. Washburne stood manfully at his post. The representatives of nearly every other foreign nation fled in dismay, fearing for their lives. The American Minister remained. Shells exploded within a few yards of his office, fires raged, great walls, pillars, and ancient monuments tottered and fell all about him, but still he would not forsake the trust which his Government had given into his keeping. From the windows of his apartments he saw all Paris in flames; he saw the streets of the great capital literally running with blood; he saw men shot down; he was saluted day and night by the hoarse yells of drunken madmen, and by the groans of the dying; but through every horror he still remained at his post.

For his heroic services during the siege of Paris and the terrible reign of the Commune, Minister Washburne received the sincere thanks of thousands of individuals whom he had aided, and of several nations and high public officers. The German Government, to subjects of which he was of untold benefit, was particularly warm in expressions of gratitude.

Mr. Washburne was practically the Prussian Minister at Paris for nearly a year; was guardian of the archives of the German Embassy, and was charged with the protection of all Germans and German interests in France during all that time.

A very considerable event in the earlier days of the siege, was the sudden appearance in Paris of Gen. Burnside, now United States Senator for Rhode Island,

12

and Paul Forbes. In one of his letters to Mr. Washburne, Bismarck was inclined to claim some credit for his liberality in allowing these two distinguished gentlemen to enter Paris, but states that " This liberality of ours has been rewarded by those excellent cigars you have been kind enough to send me."

Some time after the close of the war the Emperor Wilhelm conferred upon Mr. Washburne the Order of the Red Eagle, one of the highest within his gift, and accompanied it by a jeweled star of great value and exquisite workmanship. This, because of a constitutional provision which prohibits United States Ministers from accepting foreign orders, Mr. Washburne was compelled to decline. Still, desiring to show to him some mark of appreciation, the Emperor, on the eve of his departure for America, sent him his portrait, accompanied by a highly eulogistic letter.

After serving the United States in Paris for nearly nine years, Mr. Washburne, at the commencement of President Hayes' term of service, asked to be recalled. Returning to this country, he made his home in Chicago, and is now living in this city the quiet life of a private citizen. Still enjoying the full strength and health of robust manhood, he passes most of his time in literary pursuits. In his lofty and commodious library, surrounded by many rare engravings, books, and manuscripts in various languages, he is at all times easily accessible to those who desire to see him. His long residence at foreign conrts, among princes and grandees, has in no way changed him. He is, as he always has been, a courteous, straightforward, plain-spoken American gentleman. He is a representative American citizen who has won success by working for it. He is a living example of what greatness, under our liberal institutions, can be achieved even by those of the humblest origin. He has been highly honored by his country, and it can with all truth be said that he has deserved every honor he has received.

# DWIGHT LYMAN MOODY.

NQUESTIONABLY the foremost among the evangelists of modern times is Dwight Lyman Moody. Born on the 5th day of February, 1837, at Northfield, Mass., his parents occupying a humble position in life, he received a very limited education, but his religious training, guided by the wise counsels and fervent prayers of a loving, Christian mother, was such as to mold a nature which, in the large Christianity of its general tone, has brought comfort and heavenly peace to the hearts of tens of thousands, lowly and high born, who have listened to the simple, earnest, and unaffected exposition of the teachings of the Saviour of the world.

Mr. Moody left the place of his birth at an early age, and went to Boston. Thrown upon the world, he soon developed that self-reliant spirit and fertility of resource which has since characterized his career, and

*D. L. Moody*

distinguished him above all others as a reformer and missionary leader. Although he was a constant attendant at the Northfield Unitarian Church, upon his arrival in Boston he does not appear to have had any decided religious opinion or predilection for any particular sect or creed, because in that city he joined the Congregational Church, and identified himself with the Sabbath school of that body. Here it was that he, aided by a faithful teacher, was led to that condition of Christian hope, to give which to his fellow creatures he has labored so earnestly and diligently throughout the English-speaking world.

After a brief residence in Boston, a desire to better his condition in life induced him to come to Chicago, where he arrived about the latter part of 1855. His career here is well-known—how, by painstaking, methodical devotion to business, the sweet spirit of true Christianity permeating all his actions, he gained the confidence of his employes and the esteem of his fellows; and how, although scrupulous in his attention to business duties, he found time and opportunity to enter into religious work with that spirit of glorious enthusiasm which seems to illustrate his whole soul, and which very soon made him conspicuous in every important religious work in Chicago. An active member of the Young Men's Christian Association, he sought, and fruitfully, by untried means to bring the souls of men and women nearer to Christ, and it is well known that to his diligence and indefatigable efforts in the missionary field, the position which that institution holds to-day as a useful organization, is in no small degree to be attributed. So well did he acquit himself in the work of the society, and so deep an impression did he make in the good opinion of its members, that they finally elected him president.

In August, 1862, Mr. Moody was married to Miss Emma C. Revell, of Chicago, a lady well qualified by her tastes and talents to aid him in his work. The union is said to be a happy one, and his home is cheerful, joyous, and eminently Christian in its character.

But Mr. Moody's labors have been subject to serious interruptions and embarrassments. The great fire, which desolated the city, swept away his own happy home, and left the people he had collected around him without a church in which to worship, and deprived the children whom he loved so tenderly of the Sabbath school privileges they had learned to prize so highly. Confusion, distrust and destitution prevailed on every side. Many would have abandoned the work, but he seemed only the more resolved to prosecute it. Farwell Hall yielded to the flames, and Mr. Moody and his friends, instead of being cast down at the sight of its ashes, went energetically to work and reared upon its ruins a still more magnificent structure.

The most distinctive trait of this extraordinary man's character is his entire concentration to the work of his life. His implicit reliance upon his God smacks of the old days when Christ commanded the humble fishermen to put their trust entirely in Him, and take up the cross and preach the Gospel. This Mr. Moody has literally done. With a heroism that grace alone could inspire, he abandoned his secular calling, with all its promise of gain, and affirmed that he would devote his life to God. Remonstrances and entreaties from friends to abandon his plan were of no avail. He merely answered, " God will provide."

His idea was seconded by Mr. Ira D. Sankey, whose charming singing and rendition of the simple Christian songs have captivated the attention and filled with overwhelming emotion the souls of thousands. These two men, after laboring together in Chicago for about two years, receiving no stated salary, but merely relying upon Providence for the supply of their wants, accepted invitations to visit Europe as evangelists.

They landed at Liverpool on the 17th of June, 1873, where they unfurled the banner of the cross, and

the whole world is familiar with their remarkable success.   In London, Birmingham, Manchester, Liverpool, Glasgow, and Edinburgh, and, in fact, all over
Great Britain and Ireland, his great Christianity, his
renunciation of all priestly authority, his earnest and
simple assurance to the people that the commonest
and the highest among them could work out their own
salvation if they would, by simply, lovingly, and duti-
fully following our Saviour, requiring the mediation of
no erring man, disarmed prejudice and won the hearts
of the multitudes to Jesus.   Lords and ladies, cultured
and refined, professors high in the theology of all
times, and laborers in the hundreds of highways and
byways of life, all crowded eagerly to hear the old,
old story told in a plain, unvarnished way.

They remained abroad nearly two years.   Returning to America, after a brief period of repose, they
began work again in Northfield, Mass., on the 9th day
of September, 1875.   Their wonderful work in Britain
had prepared the way for their success at home, and
wherever they went immense audiences greeted them
with welcome and delight.

The first great meeting in this country took place at
the Brooklyn rink on Sunday, the 24th of October,
1875.   An audience of some 10,000 gathered within
the building and over 20,000 assembled outside, unable

to obtain admission. From the very first the interest was intense, and at every meeting thousands failed to obtain admission, so great was the desire of the people to attend the services. So it was with the Philadelphia meetings, which began on the 21st of November, and his work in the city of New York, beginning on the 7th of February, 1876, obtained the same results.

The religious work of these two men, both in the Eastern States and Europe, has been incalculable in its beneficial results. Bibles long closed have been reverently opened, and to-day their sacred truths gleam upon many minds with a new light. The spirit of evangelism has been quickened and developed in new and efficient ways.

In Chicago an immense tabernacle was built, capable of accommodating over 7,000 people, and this capacious building was daily filled to overflowing. As a result of these meetings, several hundred members were added to various churches in the city

And all the foregoing wonderful revivals were accomplished by a plain, uneducated, but earnest and faithful worker in the Lord's vineyard.

If you feel that you would like to travel in the same road, then study closely Mr. Moody's life, and look around you and see if there are not similar opportunities for doing good. But if you feel that you would much rather be a business man, then remember that the place you really wish for is the place you will do the most good in; for no one having a distaste for his employment will ever attain to the highest degree of success in it.

We append a sketch of "The School on the Sands," where Mr. Moody gained the training which has helped him so well during his busy life.

———

### THE SCHOOL ON THE "SANDS" IN CHICAGO.

It is nearly twenty years since Mr. Moody started the Mission Sunday-school in Chicago that was to be to him in turn a training school for his great work as an evangelist. He was then a salesman in a whole-sale boot and shoe house. On week days his steam-engine energy found full play in the effort to sell more goods than any other man in the establishment. On Sundays he worked just as hard. He rented four pews in Plymouth church, of which he was a member, and in the morning he raked boarding-houses, saloons and street corners for young men to fill them. In the afternoon he plunged into Sunday-school work. Re-cruiting was his forte. It is said that he helped build up, in turn, over a dozen different schools, as he found one after another that seemed to need his help. He stepped over denominational lines as easily in those days as now. It mattered little to him whether a school was under Methodist, Congregational, or Presbyterian management, if so be he got the gamins of the street under Sunday school influences.

His one trouble in this work was that the youngsters who needed Sunday-school instruction the most could not be persuaded to come to the ordinary school—or could not be kept there if once they were coaxed in. They were too untamed—too ill at ease among well-dressed and well-behaved children. So, more to catch the fish that slipped through the nets of the other schools than for any other reason, he decided to start a school of his own on the Sands. This was the name of a poverty-stricken, whisky-ridden, crime-steeped locality on the north side—the Five Points of Chicago.

Hiring an unfurnished room that had been last used for a saloon, he started out to drum up scholars to fill it. At first the young Arabs fought shy. Then he filled his pockets with maple sugar, and judiciously distributing it among those who promised to come, the room soon overflowed, and he was obliged to look up larger quarters. These were found in a hall over the North Market, from which the school took the name by which it was known for several years. To give an idea of the neighborhood in which the school was planted, it is said that Moody, speaking from the steps of the hall entrance could make his voice heard in the doors of 200 saloons. Here he and his helpers gathered a school that within a year had an average attendance of 650 scholars, and soon ran up to 1,000.

There was probably never another school just like it. At first there were no seats even in the room, and for some time none of the " Sunday-school requisites " of the advertisements—no blackboard, no library, no maps, no banners. But it was a live school; so thoroughly wide-awake that at first the teachers considered it a satisfactory day's work when they had been able to do a little singing and keep the turbulent membership sufficiently quiet to hear a little talking. It was a cardinal doctrine that the worse a boy was the more necessity there was of keeping him in the school. Such a confession of failure as the expulsion of a scholar was not to be thought of. Great was the ingenuity and patience required to manage some of the hard cases. There is a story of one young rough who seemed to defy all the efforts to tame him. There was danger that his riotous behavior would break up the school. Having meditated and prayed over the matter all the week, Moody came to school one Sunday persuaded that there was but one remedy that would reach his case, and that was a good thrashing.

Coming up behind the young rowdy he clasped his arms around him, lifted him from his feet and shoved him through the open door of a little ante-room. Locking the door he proceeded to business. The culprit was well endowed with muscle. But so was Moody. The excitement in the school-room was drawn off by singing until the two re-appeared, after a somewhat prolonged and noisy "interview" in the ante-room. Both were evidently well warmed up, but the result was manifest in the chastened bearing of the offender. "It was hard work," remarked Moody, "but I guess we have saved him." And they had! More than that, this exhibition of muscular Christianity was a new claim on the admiration of the school, and Moody's will was law among them thereafter. He had demonstrated his ability to keep order, and forthwith found many helpers. One day an old scholar coming up the aisle espied a raw recruit with his cap on. Snatching it off, he hit the offender a blow that sent him at full length upon the floor. "I'll learn you better than to wear your cap on in this school," was the sententious explanation as he passed on to his own seat with the air of one who was ready to do his duty.

It was not easy to find suitable teachers for the hard-bitted classes which made up such a school. And

there, as in other schools, it was not always easy to
get rid of unsuitable teachers. But a plan was hit
upon that worked to a charm. No teacher could do
such children good unless he could interest them. So
a rule was made, giving a scholar the privilege, under
certain limitations, of leaving his class when he chose
and going into another one. The result was that the
superintendent was relieved from the unpleasant task
of taking a dull teacher's class away from him. For
the class, one by one, quickly took itself away. And
thus there came about a "survival of fittest" teachers
that would have delighted Darwin himself.

Moody put a vast amount of work into the school.
His evenings and Sundays were spent in skirmishing
about the Sands, looking after old scholars and looking up new ones. He never believed that there was
anything that any sinner needed so much as he needed
the Gospel. But along with the Gospel he carried a
great deal of relief for the sick, the unemployed and
the unfortunate. He was the almoner not only of his
own charity, but of the gifts of many friends who
became interested in his work. His old employer
says that he has seen as many as twenty children come
into the store at once to be fitted out with new shoes
gratuitously.

When he finally gave up business altogether, that

he might devote all his time to missionary labor, he bought a pony to facilitate his work. Mounting it on Sunday he would go skirmishing through the streets and alleys on the search for new scholars. Coming back at the hour for school, the patient pony would sometimes be loaded, from its ears to its haunches, with ragged urchins while the later recruits hung on by the stirrups or tail!

Numerous were the conversions, wonderful the transformations that were continually occurring among these children and youth. One cold day in February, a wild lad made his appearance at the school-room door. He was clad in a man's overcoat—its rags tied together with strings. His legs were wrapped with papers, and a big pair of shoes completed his winter costume. Mr. Moody caught sight of him, gave him his hand, found him a place in a class, with as cordial and kindly attention as he could have shown the most welcome visitor. A gentleman who happened to be visiting the school that day was moved to tears by the wretched plight of the boy. After the exercises were over he took him home and gave him a full suit of clothes belonging to his own son. The boy, thus befriended, continued coming to the school, was converted, and is now a Sunday-school superintendent himself.—*Sunday-school Times.*

# GEORGE PEABODY.

GEORGE PEABODY came of an old English
family, which traced its descent back to the
year of our Lord 61, the days of the heroic
Boadicea, down through the brilliant circle of the
Knights of the Round Table, to Francis Peabody,
who in 1635 went from St. Albans, in Hertfordshire, to
the New World, and settled in Danvers, Massachusetts,
where the subject of this memoir was born one hundred and sixty years later, on the 18th of February,
1795. The parents of George Peabody were poor,
and hard work was the lot to which he was born, a lot
necessary to develop his sterling qualities of mind and
heart. He was possessed of a strong, vigorous constitution, and a quick, penetrating intellect. His education was limited, for he was taken from school at
the age of eleven, and set to earning his living. Upon
leaving school, he was apprenticed in a " country

GEORGE PEABODY.

store " in Danvers.    Here he worked hard and faithfully for four or five years.    His mind matured more
rapidly than his body, and he was a man in intellect
long before he was out of his teens.    Having gained
all the information it was possible to acquire in so
small an establishment, he began to wish for a wider
field for the exercise of his abilities.

Accordingly, he left Mr. Proctor's employment, and
spent a year with his maternal grandfather at Post
Mills village, Thetford, Vermont. " George Peabody's
year at Post Mills," says a writer who knew him,
" must have been a year of intense quiet, with good
examples always before him, and good advice whenever occasion called for it; for Mr. Dodge and his wife
were both too shrewd to bore him with it needlessly.

" It was on his return from this visit that he spent a
night at a tavern in Concord, N. H., and paid for his
entertainment by sawing wood the next morning.
That, however, must have been a piece of George's
own voluntary economy, for Jeremiah Dodge would
never have sent his grandson home to Danvers without the means of procuring the necessaries of life on
the way, and still less, if possible, would Mrs. Dodge.
· " The interest with which Mr. Peabody remembered
this visit to Post Mills is shown by his second visit so
late in life, and his gift of a library—as large a

13

library as that place needs. Of its influence on his subsequent career, of course, there is no record. Perhaps it was not much. But, at least, it gave him a good chance for quiet thinking, at an age when he needed it; and the labors of the farm may have been useful both to mind and body."

At the age of sixteen, in the year 1811, he went to Newburyport, and became a clerk in the store of his elder brother, David Peabody, who was engaged in the dry goods business at that place. He exhibited unusual capacity and promise in his calling, and soon drew upon himself the favorable attention of the merchants of the place. He was prompt, reliable, and energetic, and from the first established an enviable reputation for personal and professional integrity. It is said that he earned here the first money he ever made outside of his business. This was by writing ballots for the Federal party in Newburyport. Printed ballots had not then come into use.

He did not stay long in Newburyport, as a great fire, which burned up a considerable part of the town, destroyed his brother's store, and obliged him to seek employment elsewhere.

"The cause of Mr. George Peabody's interest in Newburyport was not alone that he had lived here for a brief period, or that his relatives had lived here;

but rather it was the warm friendship that had been shown him, which was, in fact, the basis of his subsequent prosperity. He left here in 1811, and returned in 1857. The forty-six intervening years had borne to the grave most of the persons with whom he had formed acquaintance.

"Mr. Spaulding, an old friend of his youth, had rendered him the greatest of services. When Mr. Peabody left Newburyport, he was under age, and not worth a dollar. Mr. Spaulding gave him letters of credit in Boston, through which he obtained two thousand dollars' worth of merchandise of Mr. James Reed, who was so favorably impressed with his appearance, that he subsequently gave him credit for a larger amount. This was his start in life, as he afterward acknowledged; for at a public entertainment in Boston, when his credit was good for any amount, and in any part of the world, Mr. Peabody laid his hand on Mr. Reed's shoulder, and said to those present, 'My friends, here is my first patron; and he is the man who sold me my first bill of goods.' After he was established in Georgetown, D. C., the first consignment made to him was by the late Francis Todd, of Newburyport. It was from these facts that Newburyport was always pleasant in his memory; and the donation he made to the public library was on his own suggestion, that he desired to do something of a public nature for our town."

From New England, George Peabody turned his face southward, and entered the employment of his uncle, Mr. John Peabody, who was engaged in the dry goods business in Georgetown, in the District of Columbia. He reached that place in the spring of 1812; but, as the second war with England broke out about the same time, was not able to give his immediate attention to business. His uncle was a poor man and a bad manager, and for two years the business was conducted by George Peabody, and in his own name; but at the end of that time, seeing the business threatened with ruin by his uncle's incapacity, he resigned his situation, and entered the service of Mr. Elisha Riggs, who had just established a wholesale dry goods house in Georgetown. Mr. Riggs furnished the capital for the concern, and Mr. Peabody was given the management of it. Soon after this, the latter became a partner in the house. It is said that when Mr. Riggs invited Mr. Peabody to become his partner, the latter informed him that he could not legally assume the responsibilities of the business, as he was only nineteen years old. This was no objection in the mind of the merchant, as he wanted a young and active assistant, and had discerned in his boy-manager the qualities which never fail to win success.

The new business in which he was engaged consisted chiefly in the importation and sale of European goods, and consignments of dry goods from the northern cities. It extended over a wide field, and gave Mr. Peabody a fine opportunity for the display of his abilities. He worked with energy and intelligence, and in 1815 the business was found to be so extensive that a removal to Baltimore became necessary. About this time a sort of irregular banking business was added to the operations of the house. This was chiefly the suggestion of Mr. Peabody, and proved a source of great profit

Mr. Peabody quickly took a prominent rank among the merchants of Baltimore. He was noted for " a judgment quick and cautious, clear and sound, a decided purpose, a firm will, energetic and persevering industry, punctuality and fidelity in every engagement, justice and honor controlling every transaction, and courtesy—that true courtesy which springs from genuine kindness—presiding over the intercourse of life." His business continued to increase, and in 1822 it became necessary to establish branches in Philadelphia and New York, over which Mr. Peabody exercised a careful supervision. In 1827 he went to

England on business for his firm, and during the next ten years made frequent voyages between New York and London.

In 1829 Mr. Riggs withdrew from the firm, and Mr. Peabody became the actual head of the house, the style of the firm, which had previously been " Riggs & Peabody," being changed to " Peabody, Riggs & Co."

In 1836 Mr. Peabody determined to extend his business, which was already very large, to England, and to open a branch house in London. In 1837 he removed to that city for the purpose of taking charge of his house there, and from that time London became his home.

The summer of this year was marked by one of the most terrible commercial crises the United States has ever known. "That great sympathetic nerve of the commercial world, credit," said Edward Everett, " as far as the United States was concerned, was for the time paralyzed. At that moment Mr. Peabody not only stood firm himself, but was the cause of firmness in others. There were not at that time, probably, half a dozen other men in Europe who, upon the subject of American securities, would have been listened to for a moment in the parlor of the Bank of England. But his judgment commanded respect; his integrity won back the reliance which men had been accustomed to place in American securities."

The conduct of Mr. Peabody in this crisis, placed him among the foremost merchants of London. He carried on his business upon a large scale from his base of operations in that city. He bought British manufactures in all parts of England and shipped them to the United States. His vessels brought back in return all kinds of American produce which would command a ready sale in England. Profitable as these ventures were, there was another branch of his business much more remunerative to him. The merchants and manufacturers on both sides of the Atlantic who consigned their goods to him frequently procured from him advances upon the goods long before they were sold. At other times they would leave large sums in his hands long after the goods were disposed of, knowing that they could draw whenever they needed, and that in the meanwhile their money was being so profitably invested that they were certain of a proper interest for their loans. Thus Mr. Peabody gradually became a banker, in which pursuit he was as successful as he had been as a merchant. In 1843 he withdrew from the house of Peabody, Riggs & Co., and established the house of " George Peabody & Company, of Warnford Court, City."

His dealings were chiefly with America, and in American securities, and he was always regarded as one of the best specimens of the American merchant ever seen in London. In speaking of the manner in which he organized his business establishment, he once said: "I have endeavored, in the constitution of its members and the character of its business, to make it an American house, and to give it an American atmosphere; to furnish it with American journals; to make it a center of American news, and an agreeable place for any American friends visiting London."

In the year 1851, when it was thought that there would be no representation of the achievements of American skill and industry in the Great Exhibition of that year, from lack of funds, Mr. Peabody generously supplied the sum of fifteen thousand dollars, which enabled the Commissioners to make a suitable display of the American contributions.

"He had contributed his full share, if not to the splendor, at least to the utilities of the exhibition. In fact, the leading journal at London, with a magnanimity which did it honor, admitted that England had derived more real benefit from the contributions of the United States than from those of any other country."

As has been said, Mr. Peabody made the bulk of

his colossal fortune in the banking business.  He had a firm faith in American securities, and dealt in them largely, and with confidence.  His course was now onward and upward, and each year marked an increase of his wealth.  His business operations were conducted in pursuance of a rigid system which was never relaxed.  To the very close of his life he never abandoned the exact or business-like manner in which he sought to make money.  He gave away millions with a generosity never excelled, yet he could be exacting to a penny in the fulfillment of a contract.

In his youth he contracted habits of economy, and these he retained to the last.  Being unmarried, he did not subject himself to the expense of a complete domestic establishment, but lived in chambers, and entertained his friends at his club or at a coffee-house. His habits were simple in every respect, and he was often seen making his dinner on a mutton-chop at a table laden (at his cost) with the most sumptuous and tempting viands.  His personal expenses for ten years did not average three thousand dollars per annum.

In his dress Mr. Peabody was simple and unostentatious.  He was scrupulously neat and tasteful, but there was nothing about him to indicate his vast wealth.  He seldom wore any jewelry, using merely a black band for his watch-guard.  Display of all kinds he abominated. He made several visits to his native country during his last residence in London, and commemorated each one of them by acts of princely munificence. He gave large sums to the cause of education, and to religious and charitable objects, and made each one of his near kindred wealthy. None of his relatives received less than one hundred thousand dollars, and some were given as much as three times that sum. He gave immense sums to the poor of London, and became their benefactor to such an extent that Queen Victoria sent him her portrait, which she had caused to be executed for him at a cost of over forty thousand dollars, in token of her appreciation of his services in behalf of the poor of her realm.

Mr. Peabody made another visit to the United States in 1866, and upon this occasion added large sums to many of the donations he had already made in this country. He remained here until May, 1867, when he returned to England. He came back in June, 1869, but soon sailed again for England. His health had become very feeble, and it was his belief that it would be better in the atmosphere of London, to which he had been so long accustomed. His hope of recovery was vain. He failed to rally upon reaching London, and died in that city on the 4th of

November, 1869. The news of his death created a
profound sadness on both sides of the Atlantic, for
his native and his adopted country alike revered him
as a benefactor. The Queen caused his body to be
placed in a vault in Westminster Abbey, amidst the
greatest and noblest of her kingdom, until all was in
readiness for its transportation to the United States in
a royal man-of-war. The Congress of the United
States authorized the President to make such arrange-
ments for the reception of the body as he should deem
necessary. Sovereigns, statesmen, and warriors united to do homage to the mortal remains of this plain,
simple man, who, beginning life a poor boy, and never
departing from the character of an unassuming
citizen, had made humanity his debtor by his generosity and goodness. He was borne across the ocean
with kingly honors, two great nations acting as chief
mourners, and then, when the pomp and the splendor
of the occasion were ended, they laid him down in his
native earth by the side of the mother from whom he
had imbibed those principles of integrity and goodness which were the foundation of his fame and
fortune.

It is impossible to obtain an accurate statement of
the donations made by Mr. Peabody to the objects
which enlisted his sympathy. He divided among his

relatives the sum of about three millions of dollars, giving them a portion during his last visit to this country, and leaving them the remainder at his death. He donated the immense sum of $8,470,000 to various educational and other worthy objects, over $3,000,000 of which went to the poor of London, England.

The life of such a man affords lessons full of hope and encouragement to others. In 1856, when on a visit to Danvers, now named Peabody, in honor of him, its most distinguished son and greatest benefactor, he said:

" Though Providence has granted me an unvaried and unusual success in the pursuit of fortune in other lands, I am still in heart the humble boy who left yonder unpretending dwelling. There is not a youth within the sound of my voice whose early opportunities and advantages are not very much greater than were my own, and I have since achieved nothing that is impossible to the most humble boy among you."

CORNELIUS VANDERBILT.

# CORNELIUS VANDERBILT.

EVENTY-SIX years ago, Staten Island was a mere country settlement, and its communications with the city were maintained by means of a few sail-boats, which made one trip each way per day.

One of these boats was owned and navigated by Cornelius Vanderbilt, a thriving farmer, who owned a small but well cultivated estate on Staten Island, near the present Quarantine Grounds. He was a man of exemplary character and great industry. Having a considerable amount of produce to sell in the city, he purchased a boat of his own for the purpose of transporting it thither. Frequently, residents of the island would secure passage in this boat to the city in the morning, and return with it in the evening. He realized a considerable sum of money in this way, and finally ran his boat regularly between the island and the city. This was the beginning of the New York and Staten Island Ferry. His wife was a woman of more than usual character, and aided him nobly in making his way in the world.

This admirable couple were blessed with nine children. The oldest of these, CORNELIUS, the subject of this sketch, was born at the old farm-house on Staten Island, on the 27th of May, 1794. He was a healthy, active boy, fond of all manner of out-door sports, and manifesting an unusual repugnance to the confinement and labors of the school-room. He has since declared that the only books he remembers using at school were the New Testament and the spelling-book. The result was, that he merely learned to read, write, and cipher, and that imperfectly. He was passionately fond of the water, and was never so well pleased as when his father allowed him to assist in sailing his boat. When he set himself to accomplish any thing, he was not, like most boys, deterred by the difficulties of his undertaking, but persevered until success crowned his efforts. So early did he establish his reputation for overcoming obstacles, that his boyish friends learned to regard any task which he undertook as already virtually performed.

Young Vanderbilt was always anxious to become a sailor, and, as he approached his seventeenth year, he

determined to begin life as a boatman in the harbor
of New York. On the 1st of May, 1810, he informed
his mother of his determination, and asked her to
lend him one hundred dollars to buy a boat. The
good lady had always opposed her son's wish to go to
sea, and regarded this new scheme as equally hair-
brained. As a means of discouraging him, she told
him if he would plow, harrow, and plant with corn a
certain ten-acre lot belonging to the farm, by the
twenty-seventh of that month, on which day he would
be seventeen years old, she would lend him the money.
The field was the worst in the whole farm; it was
rough, hard, and stony; but by the appointed time the
work was done, and well done, and the boy claimed
and received his money. He hurried off to a neighboring village, and bought his boat, in which he set
out for home. He had not gone far, however, when
the boat struck a sunken wreck, and filled so rapidly
that the boy had barely time to get into shoal water
before it sank.

"Undismayed at this mishap," says Mr. Parton,
from whose graphic memoir the leading incidents of
this sketch are taken, "he began his new career. His
success, as we have intimated, was speedy and great.
He made a thousand dollars during each of the next
three summers. Often he worked all night; but he was

never absent from his post by day, and he soon had
the cream of the boating business of the port.

"At that day parents claimed the services and earnings of their children till they were twenty-one.  In
other words, families made common cause against the
common enemy, Want.  The arrangement between this
young boatman and his parents was, that he should
give them all his day earnings and half his night earnings.  He fulfilled his engagement faithfully until his
parents released him from it, and with his own half of
his earnings by night, he bought all his clothes.

"He soon became the best boatman in the port.
He had no vices.  In those three years of willing
servitude to his parents, Cornelius Vanderbilt added
to the family's common stock of wealth, and gained
for himself three things—a perfect knowledge of his
business, habits of industry and self-control, and the
best boat in the harbor."

During the war of 1812, young Vanderbilt was kept
very busy.  The travel between the harbor defenses
and the city was very great, and boatmen were in
demand.

In 1813 he determined to marry.  He had wooed
and won the heart of Sophia Johnson, the daughter of
a neighbor, and he now asked his parents' consent to
his marriage, and in the winter of 1813 he was married.

His wife was a woman of unusual personal beauty and strength of character, and proved the best of partners. He has often declared since that he owed his success in life as much to her counsel and assistance as to his own efforts.

In the spring of 1814, when it was expected that New York would be attacked by a formidable British military and naval expedition, he was awarded the contract for conveying provisions from New York to the various military posts in the vicinity. This contract exempted him from military duty.

There were six posts to be supplied—Harlem, Hell Gate, Ward's Island, the Narrows, and one other in the harbor, each of which was to be furnished with one load per week. The young contractor performed all the duties of his contract at night, which left him free to attend to his boating during the day. He never failed to make a single delivery of stores, or to be absent from his post on the beach at Whitehall one single day during the whole three months. He was often without sleep, and performed an immense amount of labor during this period.

He made a great deal of money that summer, and with his earnings built a splendid little schooner, which he named the " Dread." In 1815, in connection with his brother-in-law, Captain De Forrest, he

14

built a fine schooner, called the " Charlotte," for the coasting service. She was celebrated for the beauty of her model and her great speed. During the three years succeeding the termination of the war he saved nine thousand dollars in cash, and built two or three small vessels. This was his condition in 1818.

In 1818, to the surprise and dismay of his friends, he gave up his flourishing business, in order to accept the captaincy of a steamboat which was offered him by Mr. Thomas Gibbons. The salary attached to this position was one thousand dollars. He was given command of a steamboat plying between New York and New Brunswick.

Passengers to Philadelphia, at that day, were transported by steamer from New York to New Brunswick, where they remained all night. The next morning they took the stage for Trenton, from which they were conveyed by steamer to Philadelphia. The hotel at New Brunswick was a miserable affair. When Captain Vanderbilt took command of the steamer, he was offered the hotel rent free, and accepted the offer. He placed the house in charge of his wife, under whose vigorous administration it soon acquired a great popularity.

For seven years he was harassed and hampered by the hostility of the State of New York, which had granted to Fulton and Livingston the sole right to navigate New York waters by steam. Thomas Gibbons believed this law to be unconstitutional, and ran his boats in defiance of it. The authorities of the State resented his disregard of their monopoly, and a long and vexatious warfare sprang up between them, which was ended only in 1824, by the decision of the Supreme Court of the United States in favor of Mr. Gibbons.

After the decision of the Supreme Court placed Mr. Gibbons in the full enjoyment of his rights, Captain Vanderbilt was allowed to manage the line in his own way, and conducted it with so much skill and vigor that it paid its owner an annual profit of forty thousand dollars. Mr. Gibbons offered to increase his salary to five thousand dollars, but he refused to accept the offer.

" I did it on principle," he said, afterward. " The other captains had but one thousand, and they were already jealous enough of me. Besides, I never cared for money. All I ever cared for was to carry my point."

In 1829 he determined to leave the service of Mr. Gibbons, with whom he had been connected for eleven years. He was thirty-five years old, and had saved thirty thousand dollars. He resolved to build a

steamer of his own, and command her himself, and
accordingly made known his intention to his employer.
Mr. Gibbons at once declared that he could not carry
on the line without his assistance, and told him he
might make his own terms if he would stay with him.
Captain Vanderbilt had formed his decision after
much thought, and being satisfied that he was doing
right, he persisted in his determination to set up for
himself. Mr. Gibbons then offered to sell him the
iine on the spot, and to take his pay as the money
should be earned. It was a splendid offer, but it was
firmly and gratefully refused.

After leaving Mr. Gibbons he built a small steamer,
called the " Caroline," which he commanded himself.
In a few years he was the owner of several other
small steamers plying between New York and the
neighboring towns. He made slow progress at first,
for he had strong opposition to overcome. The
steamboat interest was in the hands of powerful com-
panies, backed by immense capital. They met their
match in all cases, however, for Vanderbilt inaugurated so sharp a business opposition that the best of
them were forced to compromise with him. These
troubles were very annoying to him, and cost him
nearly every dollar he was worth, but he persevered,
and at length " carried his point."

From that time he made his way gradually in his business, until he rose to the head of the steamboat interest of the United States.

He built the famous steamer "North Star," and made a triumphal cruise in her to the Old World. He then offered the Government to carry the mails more promptly and regularly than had ever been done before, and to do this for a term of years without asking one single cent as subsidy. He was allowed to do it.

Some years ago he tried to have a bill passed consolidating the Hudson River and Harlem Railroads, and sufficient votes were promised to carry it. Unprincipled legislators, however, broke their promises, and tried to ruin him; but he found out in time to avert it, and, instead of losing, gained a large sum of money; while the men who tried to ruin him, were themselves ruined.

During the rebellion, Commodore Vanderbilt equipped his splendid steamer, the "Vanderbilt," as a man-of-war, and presented her to the Navy Department as a free gift to the nation.

He was extremely generous to his friends, and gave liberally to charitable objects. He died some few years ago, and left a family of thirteen children, nearly all of whom are still living.

# ROBERT FULTON.

R OBERT FULTON was born in the township of Little Britain (now called Fulton), in Lancaster County, Pennsylvania, in 1765. He was of Irish descent, and his father was a farmer in moderate circumstances. He was the eldest son and third child of a family of five children.

In 1766, Mr. Fulton, senior, disposed of his farm, and removed to the town of Lancaster, where he died in 1768, and there young Robert grew up under the care of his mother. He learned to read and write quickly, but did not manifest much fondness for his books after mastering his elementary studies. He early exhibited an unusual talent for drawing, however, greatly preferring the employment of his pencil to the more serious duties of the school. He displayed a remarkable talent for mechanism, which was greatly assisted by his skill in drawing, and his visits to the

ROBERT FULTON.

machine shops were always welcomed by both the apprentices and their employers, who recognized the unusual genius of the boy, and predicted great things for him in the future.

The boyhood of Fulton was passed during the stormy period of the Revolution, and in a section so close to the theater of war that he was in the midst of all the excitement engendered by the conflict. He was an ardent patriot from the first, and used his pencil freely to caricature all who showed the slightest leaning to the cause of the enemy.

In 1778, when he was thirteen years old, he bought some powder and several large sheets of pasteboard, and made rockets after his own model, for the purpose of celebrating the 4th of July.

" In the summer of 1779, Robert Fulton evinced an extraordinary fondness for inventions. He was a frequent visitor of Mr. Messersmith's and Mr. Fenno's gunsmith shops, almost daily, and endeavored to manufacture a small air-gun."

About this time he planned and completed a small working model of a fishing boat, with paddle-wheels.

Having chosen the profession of an artist and portrait painter, young Fulton removed to Philadelphia at the age of seventeen, and remained there, pursuing his vocation, until the completion of his twenty-first year.  He formed there the acquaintance of Benjamin Franklin, by whom he was much noticed. His success was rapid, and upon attaining his majority he was enabled to purchase and stock a farm of eighty-four acres in Washington County, Pennsylvania, which he gave to his mother for a home as long as she should live.  Having thus insured her comfort, he went to England for the purpose of completing his studies in his profession.  He took with him letters to Benjamin West, then at the height of his fame, and living in London.  He was cordially received by Mr. West, who was also a native of Pennsylvania, and remained an inmate of his family for several years.

Upon leaving the family of Mr. West, Fulton commenced a tour for the purpose of examining the treasures of art contained in the residences of the English nobility, and remained for two years in Devonshire.  There he became acquainted with the Duke of Bridgewater, and it is said that he was induced by this nobleman to abandon the profession of an artist, and enter upon that of a civil engineer.  Here he also met with Watt, who had just produced the steam-engine, which Fulton studied enthusiastically. His own inventive genius was not idle, and while living in Devonshire, he produced an improved mill for sawing marble, which won him the thanks and medal of the British Society for the Promotion of the Arts and Commerce; a machine for spinning flax and making ropes; and an excavator for scooping out the channels of canals and aqueducts, all of which were patented. He published a number of communications on the subject of canals in one of the leading London journals, and a treatise upon the same subject. Having obtained a patent in England for canal improvements, he went to France in 1797, with the design of introducing them in that country. He remained in Paris seven years, residing during that time with Mr. Joel Barlow, and devoting himself to the study of modern languages, and engineering and its kindred sciences.

His work was continuous and severe in Paris. He invented and painted the first panorama ever exhibited in that city, which he sold for the purpose of raising money for his experiments in steam navigation; he also designed a series of splendid colored illustrations for *The Columbiad*, the famous poem of his friend Mr. Barlow. Besides these, he invented a number of improvements in canals, aqueducts, inclined planes, boats, and guns, which yielded him considerable credit, but very little profit.

Fulton also invented a torpedo, or infernal machine, for the purpose of destroying vessels of war by approaching them under water and breaking up their hulls by the explosion. At one time, when it was thought that England would purchase Fulton's invention, it was intimated to him that he would be required to pledge himself not to dispose of it to any other power. He replied promptly:

"Whatever may be your award, I never will consent to let these inventions lie dormant should my country at any time have need of them. Were you to grant me an annuity of twenty thousand pounds, I would sacrifice all to the safety and independence of my country."

In 1806, Mr. Fulton returned to New York, and in the same year he married Miss Harriet Livingston, a niece of Chancellor Livingston, by whom he had four children. He offered his torpedo to the General Government, but the trial to which it was subjected by the Navy Department was unsuccessful for him, and the Government declined to purchase the invention.

But it was not as the inventor of engines of destruction that Robert Fulton was to achieve fame. From the time that Fulton had designed the paddle-wheels for his fishing-boat, he had never ceased to give his attention to the subject of propelling vessels by machinery, and after his acquaintance with Watt, he was more than ever convinced that the steam-engine could, under proper circumstances, be made to furnish the motive power.

It was in the face of many failures that Fulton applied himself to the task of designing a successful steamboat. During his residence in Paris he had made the acquaintance of Mr. Robert R. Livingstone, then the American minister in France, who had previously been connected with some unsuccessful steamboat experiments at home. Mr. Livingston joined heartily with him in his efforts to prove his theories by experiments, and it was finally agreed between them to build a large boat for trial on the Seine. This experimental steamer was furnished with paddle wheels, and was completed and launched early in the spring of 1803. Before it could be tried, however, the weight of the machinery carried it to the bottom of the river. He at once set to work to raise the machinery, devoting twenty-four hours, without resting or eating, to the undertaking, and succeeded in doing so, but inflicted upon his constitution a strain from which he never entirely recovered. The machinery was very slightly damaged, but it was necessary to rebuild the boat entirely. This was accomplished by July of the same year, and the boat was tried in August with triumphant success, in the presence of the French National Institute and a vast crowd of the citizens of Paris.

This steamer was very defective, but still so great an improvement upon all that had preceded it, that Messrs. Fulton and Livingston determined to build one on a larger scale in the waters of New York, the right of navigating which by steam vessels had been secured by the latter as far back as 1798. The law which granted this right had been continued from time to time through Mr. Livingston's influence, and was finally amended so as to include Fulton within its provisions. Having resolved to return home, Fulton set out as soon as possible, stopping in England on his return, to order an engine for his boat from Watt and Boulton. He gave an exact description of the engine, which was built in strict accordance with his plan, but declined to state the use to which he intended putting it.

Very soon after his arrival in New York, he commenced building his first American boat, and finding that her cost would greatly exceed his estimate, he offered for sale a third interest in the monopoly of the navigation of the waters of New York, held by Livingston and himself, in order to raise money to build the boat, and thus lighten the burdens of himself and his partner, but he could find no one willing to risk money in such a scheme. Scientific men and amateurs all agreed in pronouncing Fulton's scheme impracticable; but he went on with his work, his boat attracting no less attention and exciting no less ridicule than the ark had received from the scoffers in the days of Noah. The steam-engine ordered from Boulton and Watt was received in the latter part of 1806; and in the following spring the boat was launched from the ship-yard of Charles Brown, on the East River. Fulton named her the " Clermont," after the country seat of his friend and partner, Chancellor Livingston. She was one hundred and sixty tons burthen, one hundred and thirty feet long, eighteen feet wide, and seven feet deep. Her engine was made with a single cylinder, two feet in diameter, and of four feet stroke; and her boiler was twenty feet long, seven feet deep, and eight feet broad. The diameter of the paddle-wheels was fifteen feet, the boards four feet long, and dipping two feet in the water. The boat was completed about the last of August, and she was moved by her machinery from the East River into the Hudson, and over to the Jersey shore. This trial, brief as it was, satisfied Fulton of its success, and he announced that in a few days the steamer would sail from New York for Albany. A few friends, including several scientific men and mechanics, were invited to take passage in the boat, to witness her performance; and they accepted the invitation with a general conviction that they were to do but little more than witness another failure.

Monday, September 10, 1807, came at length, and a vast crowd assembled along the shore of the North River to witness the starting. Precisely at one o'clock —the hour for sailing—the moorings were thrown off, and the "Clermont" moved slowly out into the stream. In a little while she was fairly under weigh, and making a steady progress up the stream at the rate of five miles per hour. Fulton soon discovered that the paddles were too long, and took too deep a hold on the water, and stopped the boat for the purpose of shortening them.

Having remedied this defect, the "Clermont" continued her voyage during the rest of the day and all night, without stopping, and at one o'clock the next day ran alongside the landing at Clermont, the seat of Chancellor Livingston. She lay there until nine the next morning, when she continued her voyage toward Albany, reaching that city at five in the afternoon, having made the entire distance between New York and Albany (one hundred and fifty miles) in thirty-two hours of actual running time, an average speed of nearly five miles per hour. On her return trip, she

reached New York in thirty hours running time—
exactly five miles per hour. Fulton states that during
both trips he encountered a head wind. She continued to ply regularly between New York and Albany
until the close of navigation for that season, always
carrying a full complement of passengers, and more or
less freight. During the winter she was overhauled
and enlarged, and her speed improved. In the spring
of 1808 she resumed her regular trips, and since then
steam navigation on the Hudson has not ceased for a
single day, except during the closing of the river by
ice.

In 1811 and 1812, Fulton built two steam ferry-
boats for the North River, and soon after added a third
for the East River. These boats were the beginning of
the magnificent steam ferry system which is to-day one
of the chief wonders of New York.

Early in 1814, the city of New York was seriously
menaced with an attack from the British fleet, and
Fulton, at the request of a committee of citizens, prepared plans for a vessel of war to be propelled by
steam, capable of carrying a strong battery, with
furnaces for red-hot shot, and which, he represented,
would move at the rate of four miles an hour. In
March, 1814, Congress authorized the building of one
or more floating batteries after the plan presented by

Fulton.   Her keel was laid on the 20th of June, 1814,
and on the 31st of October of the same year, she was
launched, amid great rejoicings, from the ship-yard of
Adam and Noah Brown.   In May, 1815, her engines
were put on board, and on the 4th of July of that
year she made a trial trip to Sandy Hook and back,
accomplishing the round trip—a distance of fifty-three
miles—in eight hours and twenty minutes, under steam
alone.   Before this, however, peace had been pro-
claimed, and Fulton had gone to rest from his labors.
The ship was a complete success, and was the first
steam vessel of war ever built.

Fulton followed up the "Clermont," in 1807, with a
larger boat, called the "Car of Neptune," which was
placed on the Albany route as soon as completed.
In 1809 Fulton obtained his first patent from the
United States; and in 1811 he took out a second
patent for some improvement in his boats and machinery.   His patents were limited to the simple
means of adapting paddle wheels to the axle of the
crank of Watt's engine.

He died on the 24th of February, 1815, at the age
of fifty years.   He left a widow and four children.
By the terms of his will he bequeathed to his wife an
income of nine thousand dollars a year, and five hundred dollars to each of his children until they were

twelve years old, after which they were each to receive
one thousand dollars a year until they should attain
the age of twenty-one years.

In person, Fulton was tall and handsome.    His
manner was polished, cordial, and winning.   He made
friends rapidly, and never failed in his efforts to enlist
capital and influence in support of his schemes.    He
was manly, fearless, and independent in character, and
joined to a perfect integrity a patience and indomi-
table resolution which enabled him to bear up under
every disappointment, and which won him in the end
a glorious success.

15

# GEN. JAS. A. GARFIELD.

IT has been observed by an eminent philosopher that some men make themselves great, and some men have greatness thrust upon them. While the presidential nomination fell upon General Garfield with all the suddenness of the lighning bolt to which it is so often likened, it is the only stroke of pure good fortune that ever fell to him. His success, his position before the country, were the results of his untiring industry and his sturdy sense of duty. He never had the advantages of wealth nor of family connections, and he kept himself in Congress for seventeen years by a popularity based on his character and his legitimate work as a legislator, and not by artifice or trimming.

James Abram Garfield was born in Orange, Cuyahoga County, Ohio, fifteen miles from Cleveland, Nov. 10, 1831. His father was a farmer in moderate

J. A. Garfield

circumstances, and died when James was only two years old. There were three other children.

All the children had to work hard, as the widow had but scanty means of support for her family. James worked on the farm in summer and in a carpenter's shop in the winter. Finding that he could make better wages working on the Ohio canal, he secured employment first as driver on the towpath and afterward as helmsman. He intended at one time to ship as a seaman on a lake vessel, but his plans were changed by a fit of sickness, and his intentions were turned in another direction. He had from early boyhood felt a very keen desire for an education, and had been laboriously saving money to enable him to go to school. After recovering from the fit of sickness just referred to, he became a pupil of the Geanga academy, near his home. His mother was able to let him have a little money, and this she supplemented with some provisions and cooking utensils, and he boarded himself at school. After this start that his mother gave him, he never called on her for assistance. He spent all his odd hours at the carpenter's bench, taught school winters, and thus managed to support himself, attend the regular terms of the academy, and save some money for a college education. Having a very retentive memory, he learned with comparative ease.

A reminiscence of his earlier manhood is found in the recital given by one Capt. Stiles, the present sheriff of Ashtabula County, Ohio.  In 1850, Capt. Stiles relates, Garfield taught the district school of Stiles' district, and " boarded around."  Like many other school-masters of pioneer days, Garfield's wardrobe was scanty, consisting of but one suit of blue jean. One day the schoolmaster was so unfortunate as to rend his pantaloons across the knee in an unseemly degree.  He pinned up the rend as best he could, and went to the homestead of the Stiles' where he was then. boarding.  Good Mrs. Stiles cheeringly said to the unfortunate pedagogue, " Oh, well, James, never mind; you go to bed early and I will put a nice patch under that tear and darn it up all nice so that it will last all winter, and when you get to be United States Senator, nobody will ask you what kind of clothes you wore when you were keeping school."  When Gen. Garfield was elected Senator from the State of Ohio, Mrs. Stiles, who is still a hale old lady, sent her congratulations to him and reminded him of the torn pantaloons; and for her kindly congratulations she received a most touching reply from the newly elected Senator, assuring her that the incident was fresh in his memory.

At the age of 23 years he had education enough to

enter the junior class at college, and money enough to support him at college for a year. He borrowed enough money to support him another year, and in 1854 he entered the junior class of Williams College. In 1856 he graduated with honors.

When Garfield returned to Ohio, he obtained the Professorship of Latin and Greek in the little college at Hiram, Portage County, Ohio. He devoted himself assiduously not only to the instruction of his classes, but to the better establishment of the college, and he had not been professor two years when he was made president. The college was under the control of the Campbellite denomination, a body with which he had connected himself before going to college. As president of the college he pursued his own studies while teaching others, constantly adding to his stock of information. The Campbellites have no ordained ministry, and on Sundays President Garfield often addressed the congregations of his denomination, but he never contemplated devoting himself to the ministry as a regular thing. His preaching was merely incidental.

While a professor of Greek and Latin, Gen. Garfield was very happily married to Miss Lucretia Rudolph, daughter of a neighboring farmer. As a girl, she was quiet, thoughtful, refined. As a woman, her qualities of mind, as well as of heart, have contributed materially to her husband's successful career. Several children were born to Gen. and Mrs. Garfield, two of whom have died. Harry and James, the two oldest children, are now strong young men. Molly, the only daughter, is a young lady. The youngest children are two boys, Irwin and Abram.

The General's political career began in 1859. He was elected at that time to the State Senate, but did not resign his college presidency, having no idea then of a public career. But the war came to alter all his plans. During the winter of 1861 he was active in the passage of measures for arming the State militia, and his eloquence and energy made him a conspicuous leader of the Union party. Early in the summer of 1861, he was elected Colonel of an infantry regiment (the 42d) raised in Northern Ohio, many of the soldiers in which had been students at Hiram. He took the field in Eastern Kentucky, was soon put in command of a brigade, and by making one of the hardest marches ever made by recruits, surprised and routed the rebel forces, under Humphrey Marshal, at Piketon.

From Eastern Kentucky Gen. Garfield was transferred to Louisville, and from that place hastened to

join the army of Gen. Buell, which he reached with
his brigade in time to participate in the second day's
fighting at Pittsburg Landing.   He took part in the
siege of Corinth, and in the operations along the
Memphis and Charleston railroad.   In January, 1863,
he was appointed chief of staff of the army of the
Cumberland, and bore a prominent share in all the
campaigns in middle Tennessee in the spring and
summer of that year.   His last conspicuous military
service was at the battle of Chickamauga.   For his
conduct in that battle he was promoted to a Major-
Generalship.

General Garfield was nominated for Congress in
1862, while he was in the field, without asking his consent.   When he heard of the nomination, Garfield re-
flected that it would be fifteen months before the
Congress would meet to which he would be elected,
and believing, as did everyone else, that the war could
not possibly last a year longer, concluded to accept.

He remained in the field till his term of office
began, and, the war being then in progress, expressed
considerable regret that he had accepted the election.

On entering Congress, in December, 1863, General
Garfield was placed upon the committee on military
affairs, with Schenck and Farnsworth, who were also
fresh from the field.   He took an active part in the

debates of the House, and won a recognition which few new members succeeded in gaining. He was not popular among his fellow-members during his first term. They thought him something of a pedant because he sometimes showed his scholarship in his speeches, and they were jealous of his prominence. His solid attainments and amiable social qualities enabled him to overcome this prejudice during his second term, and he became on terms of close friendship with the best men in both Houses. His committee service during his second term was on the ways and means, which was quite to his taste, for it gave him an opportunity to prosecute the studies in finance and political economy which he had always felt a fondness for. He was a hard worker and a great reader in those days, going home with his arms full of books from the Congressional library, and sitting up late nights to read them. It was then that he laid the foundations of the convictions on the subject of national finance which he uniformly held to firmly amid all the storms of political agitation. He was renominated in 1864, without opposition; but in 1866 Mr. Hutchins, whom he had supplanted, made an effort to defeat him. Hutchins canvassed the district thoroughly, but the convention nominated Garfield by acclamation. Thereafter he had no opposition in his own party. In 1872 the Liberals and Democrats united to beat him, but his majority was larger than ever. In 1874 the Greenbackers and Democrats combined and put up a popular soldier against him, but they made no impression on the result.

When James G. Blaine went to the Senate, in 1877, the mantle of Republican leadership in the House was by common consent placed upon Garfield, and he wore it with honor.

In January, 1880, General Garfield was elected to the Senate to the seat which was vacated by Allen G. Thurman on the 4th of March, 1881. He received the unanimous vote of the Republican caucus, an honor never given to any other man of any party in the State of Ohio.

General Garfield acquired a large influence in Congress, and commanded the respect of both parties, as few other men did. This respect was based on an open, cordial disposition, and the universally acknowledged sincerity and ability of the man. He was notable for his studious and methodical habits. He was found on one occasion in the Congressional library, poring over a table full of editions of Horace, and critical works regarding that poet. He explained his occupation by saying that he found he was overworked, and he was resting himself by applying his mind to subjects having no connection with his Congressional duties.

What a grand scene was that in the Senate chamber, in the great rotunda, and on the porch of the Capitol, when General Garfield took the oath of office and delivered his inaugural address! He was calm and firm in all his movements before the assembled thousands, and his voice was clear and strong as he read his recommendations concerning a better civil service. How little did he know that he must give his life for those principles, before the people could be made to realize the situation.

Among the thousands of persistent hunters for office who followed General Garfield and intruded themselves upon his notice, was Charles J. Guiteau. He was born in Freeport, Illinois, and was by profession a lawyer. He was not long in the practice of law, owing to the fact that in Chicago and New York, the only places where he opened an office he was unable to obtain business. He seems to have been from earliest boyhood an erratic, self-willed, cruel character. He dogged the President's footsteps seeking office, and mortified at his failure he determined to have revenge. Various schemes suggested themselves to him, according to his own confession, which would bring disgrace and failure upon the administration and shame upon the President, but none would or could satisfy him but the murder of General Garfield. Arming himself with a heavy revolver, he determined to obtain his revenge by shooting the President. On Friday, the 1st day of July, 1881, Guiteau saw by the papers that the President intended to take the train for New York the next morning. On the morning of July 2d he loaded his revolver and quietly waited at the railway station for his victim. The President passed him and he fired the first shot. He was so close to his victim that he saw that his aim had not been true, and as the startled President leaped one side the assassin took a surer aim and fired the second time with deadly effect. The awful calamity was telegraphed to all parts of the world, striking horror to all hearts. After months of heroic, patient suffering, the President expired peacefully and calmly.

Everywhere there was weeping, and the messages of condolence which came to Mrs. Garfield were as sincere as they were numerous. One of the first received was from the Queen of England, and read as follows :—

BALMORAL.

"Words cannot express the deep sympathy I feel with you. May God support and comfort you, as He alone can.

"Signed THE QUEEN."

Towns, cities, and states, republics and kingdoms, including nearly every nation on earth, sent their messages of sympathy. The exhibition of a grief so world-wide was a sublime event, and something new in the world's history.

# ELIAS HOWE.

LIAS HOWE was born in the town of Spencer, Massachusetts, in 1819. He was one of eight children. His father was a farmer and miller, and, as was the custom at that time in the country towns of New England, carried on in his family some of those minor branches of industry suited to the capacity of children, with which New England abounds. When Elias was six years old, he was set, with his brothers and sisters, to sticking wire teeth through the leather straps used for making cotton cards. When he became old enough, he assisted his father in his saw-mill and grist-mill, and during the winter months picked up a meager education at the district school. He was not fitted for hard work, however, as he was frail in constitution and incapable of bearing much fatigue. Moreover, he inherited a species of lameness which proved a great obstacle to any undertaking on his part, and gave him no little trouble all through life. At the age of eleven he went to live out on the farm of a neighbor, but the labor proving too severe for him, he returned home and resumed his place in his father's mills, where he remained until he was sixteen years old.

When at this age, he conceived an ardent desire to go to Lowell to seek his fortune. Obtaining his father's consent, he went there, and found employment as a learner in one of the large cotton mills of the city. He remained there two years, when the great financial disaster of 1837 threw him out of employment and compelled him to look for work elsewhere. He obtained a place at Cambridge, in a machine-shop, and was put to work upon the new hemp-carding machinery of Professor Treadwell.

Howe remained in Cambridge only a few months, however, and was then given a place in the machine-shop of Ari Davis, of Boston.

At the age of twenty-one he married. This was a rash step for him, as his health was very delicate, and his earnings were but nine dollars per week. Three children were born to him in quick succession, and he found it no easy task to provide food, shelter and clothing for his little family. The light-heartedness for which he had formerly been noted entirely deserted him, and he became sad and melancholy. His health did not improve, and it was with difficulty that he could perform his daily task. His strength was so slight that he would frequently return home from his day's work too much exhausted to eat. He could only go to bed, and in his agony he wished " to lie in bed forever and ever." Still he worked faithfully and conscientiously, for his wife and children were very dear to him; but he did so with a hopelessness which only those who have tasted the depths of poverty can understand.

About this time he heard it said that the great necessity of the age was a machine for doing sewing, and it was conceded by all who thought of the matter at all, that the man who could invent such a machine would make a fortune. Howe's poverty inclined him to listen to these remarks with great interest. He set to work to achieve the task, and, as he knew well the dangers which surround an inventor, kept his own counsel. He watched his wife as she sewed, and his first effort was to devise a machine which should do what she was doing. He made a needle pointed at both ends, with the eye in the middle, that should work up and down through the cloth, and carry the thread through at each thrust; but his elaboration of this conception would not work satisfactorily. It was not until 1844, over a year after he began the attempt to invent the machine, that he conceived the idea of using two threads, and forming a stitch by the aid of a shuttle and a curved needle with the eye near the point. This was the triumph of his skill. Satisfied that he had at length solved the problem, he constructed a rough model of his machine of wood and wire, in October, 1844, and operated it to his perfect satisfaction.

At this time, he had abandoned his work as a journeyman mechanic, and had removed to his father's house. His father had established in Cambridge a machine-shop for the cutting of strips of palm-leaf used in the manufacture of hats. Elias and his family lived under his father's roof, and in the garret of the house the half-sick inventor put up a lathe, where he did a little work on his own account, and labored on his sewing-machine. He was miserably poor, and could scarcely earn enough to provide food for his family; and, to make matters worse, his father, who was disposed to help him, lost his shop and its contents by fire. Poor Elias was in a most deplorable condition. · He had his model in his head, and was fully satisfied of its excellence, but he had not the money to buy the materials needed in making a perfect machine, which would have to be constructed of steel and iron, and without which he could not hope to convince others of its value. His great invention was useless to him without the five hundred dollars which he needed in the construction of a working model.

In this dilemma, he applied to a friend, Mr. George Fisher, a coal and wood merchant of Cambridge, who was a man of some means. He explained his invention to him, and succeeded in forming a partnership with him. Fisher agreed to take Howe and his family to board with him while the latter was making the machine, to allow his garret to be used as a workshop, and to advance the five hundred dollars necessary for the purchase of tools and the construction of a model. In return for this he was to receive one-half of the patent, if Howe succeeded in patenting his machine. About the first of December, 1844, Howe and his family accordingly moved into Fisher's house, and the little workshop was set up in the garret. He worked all day, and sometimes nearly all night, and in April, 1845, had his machine so far advanced that he sewed a seam with it. By the middle of May the machine was completed, and in July he sewed with it the seams of two woolen suits, one for himself and the other for Mr. Fisher. The sewing was so well done that it outlasted the cloth.

Having patented his machine, Howe endeavored to bring it into use. He first offered it to the tailors of Boston; but they, while admitting its usefulness, told him it would never be adopted by their trade, as it would ruin them. Other efforts were equally unsuccessful. Every one admitted and praised the ingenuity of the machine, but no one would invest a dollar in it. Fisher became disgusted, and withdrew from his partnership, and Howe and his family moved back to his father's house. Thoroughly disheartened, he abandoned his machine. He then obtained a place as engineer on a railroad, and drove a locomotive until his health entirely broke down.

With the loss of his health his hopes revived, and he determined to seek in England the victory which he had failed to win here. Unable to go himself, he sent his machine by his brother Amasa, in October, 1846. There he found Mr. William Thomas, of Cheapside, London, and explained to him his brother's invention. Mr. Thomas offered the sum of twelve hundred and fifty dollars for the machine which Amasa Howe had brought with him, and agreed to pay Elias fifteen dollars per week if he would enter his service, and adapt the machine to his business of umbrella and corset making. Elias accepted the offer, and, upon his brother's return to the United States,

16

sailed for England. He remained in Mr. Thomas's employ for about eight months, and at the end of that time left him, having found him hard, exacting, and unreasonable.

Meanwhile his sick wife and three children had joined him in London, and he had found it hard to provide for them on the wages given him by Mr. Thomas; but after being thrown out of employment his condition was desperate indeed. He was in a strange country, without friends or money, and often he and his little family went whole days without food. Their sufferings were very great, but at length Howe was able (probably by assistance from home) to send his family back to his father's house. He himself remained in London, still hoping to bring his machine into use. It was in vain, however, and so, collecting what few household goods he had acquired in England, he shipped them to America, and followed them thither himself in another vessel, pawning his model and patent papers to pay his passage. When he landed in New York he had half a crown in his pocket, and there came to him on the same day a letter telling him that his wife was dying with consumption in Cambridge. He was compelled to wait several days, as he was too feeble to walk, until he could obtain the money for his fare to Cambridge, but at length succeeded in reaching that place just in time to see his wife die. In the midst of his grief he received the announcement that the vessel containing the few household goods which he had shipped from England had been lost at sea. It seemed to him that Fate was bent upon destroying him, so rapid and stunning were the blows she dealt him.

Soon after his return home, however, he obtained profitable employment, and, better still, discovered that his machine had become famous during his absence. Fac-similes of it had been constructed by unscrupulous mechanics, who paid no attention to the patents of the inventor, and these copies had been exhibited in many places as "wonders," and had even been adopted in many important branches of manufacture. Howe at once set to work to defend his rights. He found friends to aid him, and in August, 1850, began those famous suits which continued for four years, and were at length decided in his favor.

In 1850, Howe removed to New York, and began in a small way to manufacture machines to order. He was in partnership with a Mr. Bliss, but for several years the business was so unimportant that upon the death of his partner, in 1855, he was enabled to buy out that gentleman's interest, and thus become the sole proprietor of his patent. Soon after this his business began to increase, and continued until his own proper profits and the royalty which the courts compelled other manufacturers to pay him for the use of his invention grew from $300 to $200,000 per annum. In 1867, when the extension of his patent expired, it is stated that he had earned a total of two millions of dollars by it. It cost him large sums to defend his rights, however, and he was very far from being as wealthy as was commonly supposed, although a very rich man.

In the Paris Exposition of 1867, he exhibited his machines, and received the gold medal of the Exposition, and the Cross of the Legion of Honor in addition, as a compliment to him as a manufacturer and inventor.

He contributed money liberally to the aid of the Union in the late war, and enlisted as a private soldier in the Seventeenth Regiment of Connecticut Volunteers. He died at Brooklyn, Long Island, on the 3d of October, 1867.

HIRAM POWERS.

# HIRAM POWERS.

IRAM POWERS was born in Woodstock, Vermont, on the 29th of July, 1805. He was the eighth in a family of nine children, and was the son of a farmer who found it hard to provide his little household with the necessaries of life. He grew up as most New England boys do, sound and vigorous in health, passing the winters in attendance upon the district schools, and the summers in working on the farm. "The only distinctive trait exhibited by the child was mechanical ingenuity; he excelled in caricature, was an adept in constructiveness, having made countless wagons, windmills, and weapons for his comrades, attaining the height of juvenile reputation as the inventor of what he called a 'patent fuse.'"

His father was induced to become security for one of his friends, and, as frequently happens, lost all he had in consequence. Following close upon this disaster came a dreadful famine in the State, caused **by** an almost total failure of the crops.

One of the sons had managed to secure an education at Dartmouth College, and had removed to Cincinnati, where he was at this time editing a newspaper. Thither his father, discouraged by the famine, determined to follow him. Accordingly, placing his household goods and his family in three wagons, and being joined by another family, he set out on the long journey to the West. This was in 1819, when young Hiram was fourteen years old. In due time they reached the Ohio River, down which stream they floated on a flatboat until they came to Cincinnati, then a city of fourteen thousand inhabitants.

Through the assistance of his eldest son, the editor, Mr. Powers was enabled to secure a farm not far from Cincinnati, and removing his family to it, began the task of clearing and cultivating it. Unfortunately for the new-comers, the farm was located on the edge of a pestilential marsh, the poisonous exhalations of which soon brought the whole family down with the ague. Mr. Powers the elder died from this disease, and Hiram was ill and disabled from it for a whole year. The family was broken up and scattered, and our hero, incapable of performing hard work so soon after his sickness, obtained a place in a produce store in Cincinnati, his duty being to watch the principal road by which the farmers' wagons, laden with grain and corn whisky, came into the city, and to inform the men in charge of them that they could obtain bet- ter prices for their produce from his employers than from any other merchant in the city. It was also a part of his duty to help to roll the barrels from the wagons to the store. He made a very good "drum- mer," and gave satisfaction to his employers, but as the concern soon broke up, he was again without em- ployment.

His brother, the editor, now came to his assistance, and made a bargain with the landlord of a hotel in the city to establish a reading-room at his hotel. The landlord was to provide the room and obtain a few paying subscribers ; the editor was to stock it with his exchange newspapers, and Hiram was to be put in charge of it and receive what could be made by it. The reading-room was established, but as the landlord failed to comply with his agreement, Powers was forced to abandon the undertaking.

About that time, a clock-maker and organ-builder employed him to collect bad debts in the country. He succeeded so well that his employer offered to give him a place in the factory, saying there would always be plenty of rough work at which an inexperienced hand could employ himself. His first task was to thin down with a file some brass plates which were to be used as parts of the stops of an organ. Powers was expected to do merely the rough work, after which the plates were to pass into the hands of the regular finisher. His employer, knowing that the task was one which would require time, told him he would look in in a few days, and see how he had succeeded. The young man's mechanical talent, on which he had prided himself when a boy in Vermont, now did him good service, and he applied himself to his task with skill and determination. When his employer asked for the plates, he was astonished to find that Powers had not only done the rough work, but had finished them much better than the regular finisher had ever done, and this merely by his greater nicety of eye and his undaunted energy. He had blistered his hands terribly, but had done his work well. His employer was delighted, and, finding him so valuable an assistant, soon gave him the superintendence of all his machinery, and took him to live in his own family.

Powers displayed great skill in the management of the mechanical department of the business, and this, added to the favor shown him by the "boss," drew upon him the jealousy of the other workmen. In face of the ridicule of the workmen, he invented a ma

chii : for cutting out wooden clock wheels, in consideration of which he received an old silver bull's-
eye watch.

Soon after this, in a chance visit to the Museum in
Cincinnati, he saw a plaster cast of Houdon's "Washington." It was the first bust he had ever seen, and
he : ays it moved him strangely. He had an intense
desire to know how it was done, and a vague consciousness that he could do work of the same kind if
he could find an instructor. The instructor he soon
found in a German living in the city, who made
plaster casts of busts, and from him he learned the
secret of the art. He proved an apt pupil, and surprised his teacher by his proficiency.

The true principles of his art seemed to come to
him naturally, and having the genius to comprehend
them so readily, he had the courage to hold on to
them often in the face of adverse criticism. While
conscious of having a perfectly correct eye, however,
he did not scorn the humbler method of obtaining
( tactness by mathematical measurement.

He did not regularly devote himself to his art, however, but remained in the employment of the organ
and clock maker for some time longer, giving his
leisure hours to constant practice. When he was
about twenty-three years old. a Frenchman. owning a

museum of natural history and wax figures, induced him to become "inventor, wax-figure maker, and general mechanical contriver" in the museum. Powers remained in his employ for seven years, hoping all the while to earn money enough to devote himself entirely to art, which had now become his great ambition. He had married in this interval, and had a wife and children to support.

Powers was now thirty years old and had acquired considerable reputation in Cincinnati as an artist. His abilities coming to the notice of Mr. Nicholas Longworth, of that city, that good genius of young men of talent called on him and offered to buy out the museum and establish him in the business. The offer was declined with thanks. Mr. Longworth then proposed to send him to Italy to study his profession, but this, too, being declined, Mr. Longworth urged him to go to Washington and try his fortune with the public men of the country. To this Powers consented, and, aided by his generous friend, he repaired to the national capital in 1835, and spent two years there. During this period he modeled busts of Andrew Jackson, J. Q. Adams, Calhoun, Chief Justice Marshall, Woodbury, Van Buren, and others. Being unable to secure a model of Webster in Washington, the statesman invited him to go to Marshfield for that purpose.

Powers accepted the invitation, and declares that he
looks back upon his sojourn there as one of the most
delightful portions of his life.

General Jackson was very kind to him, and won his
lasting esteem and gratitude.

One of his sitters in Washington was Senator
Preston, of South Carolina, who conceived such an
interest in him that he wrote to his brother, General
Preston, of Columbia, South Carolina, a gentleman of
great wealth, urging him to come to the artist's assistance, and send him to Italy. General Preston at once
responded to this appeal, of which Powers was ignorant, and wrote to the artist to draw on him for a
thousand dollars, and go to Italy at once, and to draw
on him annually for a similar sum for several years.
Powers was profoundly touched by this noble offer,
and accepted it as frankly as it had been made. He
sent his models to Italy, and took his departure for
the Old World in 1837. Speaking of Mr. Preston's
generosity, he said, some years ago: "I have endeavored to requite his kindness by sending him works
of mine, equal in money value to his gifts; but I can
never extinguish my great obligations. I fear he don't
like me since the war—for I could not suppress my
strong national feelings for any man's friendship—
but I like and honor him : J would do anything

in my power to show him my inextinguishable gratitude."

He reached Florence in advance of his models, and
while waiting for them made two busts, one of a professor in Harvard College, and the other of an American lady.    A severe domestic affliction, however,
which came upon him soon after his arrival in Italy,
affected him so greatly that he was not able to return
to his work for a long time.    Then he applied himself
to his busts, which were warmly praised by the artists
in Florence and by his countrymen traveling abroad.
Thorwaldsen visited him in his studio, and pronounced
his bust of Webster the best work of its kind in modern times, and praises from other distinguished artists
were equally as warm.    Orders came in rapidly from
English and Italians, and from Americans in Europe,
and the sculptor soon had as much business as he
could attend to.    He gave his leisure time to work on
an ideal figure, which, when completed, was purchased
by an English gentleman of wealth.    This was " The
Greek Slave," the most popular of all his works.
Duplicates of it were exhibited in America and at the
Crystal Palace in England, and won him praise from
all quarters.    This single work established his fame as
an artist, and brought him orders from all parts of the
civilized world.    His statue of " Eve," which had

preceded "The Greek Slave" by a year, had been pronounced by Thorwaldsen fit to be any man's masterpiece, but it had not created such a furore as "The Greek Slave." Subsequently he made an exquisite bust of the Grand Duchess of Tuscany, with which the Grand Duke was so pleased that he called on Powers, and asked him as a favor to himself to apply to him whenever he could do him a service. Powers asked permission to take a cast of the Venus, and this much-coveted boon, which had been denied to other artists for years, was at once granted to him.

Since then his works have been numerous. Among these are "The Fisher Boy," of which three duplicates in marble have been made; "Il Penseroso;" "Proserpine," a bust; "California;" "America," modeled for the Crystal Palace at Sydenham, England; "Washington" and "Calhoun," portrait statues, the former for the State of Louisiana, and the latter for the State of South Carolina; and "Benjamin Franklin" and "Thomas Jefferson," in the Capitol at Washington. His works are all marked by beauty and vigor of conception as well as by exquisite finish. Beautiful as his ideal figures are, he yet excels in his busts and statues of the great men of his native land. His "Jefferson" and "Franklin" are wonderful works, and his "Calhoun" is said to be almost life-like. This last was wrecked on the coast of Long Island on its voyage to America, and remained in the sea for some time, but being well packed, was found, when raised, to be only slightly damaged by the water.

Mr. Powers resided in Italy for many years, and his studio was a favorite resort of young artists.

He died several years ago, revered and honored by the whole world.

JAY GOULD.

# JAY GOULD.

---

"Some are born great, some achieve greatness, and some have greatness thrust upon them."—*Shàkespeare.*

N most of the countries of Europe, and especially in England, great wealth, when uninherited, is, as a general thing, realized through the slow and patient channels of some trade or calling. This, doubtless, is owing to the fact, that the natural resources of these countries are mainly developed to their utmost capacity, and that so narrow are their boundaries, individually, as well as their ideas of government, the spirit of enterprise can find no resting place for the sole of its foot among the impoverished masses of their dense populations.

When, however, we come to contrast this undesirable state of things with the condition of affairs within the boundaries of our own vast commonwealth, we are at once struck with the magnitude of their dissimilarity.

Here a newly created world, so to speak, possessed of wealth far exceeding that of "Ormus, and of Ind," and teeming with all the resources necessary to our greatness and happiness, lies spread out before us in boundless expanses, presenting to every species of enterprise fields for operation so filled with promise, and of such gigantic magnitude, that those of the Old World are dwarfed into utter insignificance before them. Under such circumstances it is not a matter of surprise that our vast resources are becoming rapidly developed, that cities and civilizations are now being scattered through regions not long since sacred to the foot of the red man, and that constantly in our midst some adventurous and far-seeing spirit leaps from out the masses, and, at a single bound, as it were, attains to colossal wealth and importance.

There is no stronger case in point touching this latter relation than that presented by the gentleman whose name appears at the head of this article, and who has for some time past commanded so large a share of the public attention with regard to the boldness and magnitude of his operations in some of the leading interests of our economy.

Jay Gould was born in Roxbury, Delaware County, a rude part of Western New York, May 27, 1837; so he is not yet 46. Indeed, his coal-black beard and hair, which, though thin, is scarcely touched with gray, indicate a man below middle life.

His father, John B. Gould, was a poor farmer, and could scarcely earn enough to support his large family in the simplest style. The boy was the youngest, and, when at the age of 10 or 12 his great thirst for knowledge developed, his elder sisters, young ladies of considerable culture, became his teachers. Young Gould, however, early betrayed symptoms of genius and self-reliance, for he had scarcely got well into his school days till he regarded himself already a man, and invented a mouse trap. This latter has been considered by some as either a bitter sarcasm upon the unwieldy dimensions of the great, square, unsightly white frame house in which he was born, or a graphic foreshadowing of his subsequent operations in Wall street.

His boyhood in Roxbury was about the same as that of other boys roundabout. He worked around the farm, planting and hoeing, going to district school some, doing chores and milking cows nights, and about the most vivid memory of that time is of an old brindle cow that he tried to milk. She kicked

him in the most skillful manner, and he turned a complete somerset in the yard.  " It seems funnier now
than it did then," he said.

The growing boy studied nights, read all the books
he could get in that sparsely-settled country, and at
the age of fourteen appealed to his father to send him
to the academy in the adjoining town.  His father
could not afford it.  The boy thought it over deliber-
ately, felt that his study of mathematics, now beyond
the instruction of Roxbury, must be gratified some-
how, and resolved to go to the academy and pay his
own expenses.  He asked his father's permission.
" Of course you can go if you want to," was the natural reply; " you ain't good for much here."  It was
the solemn truth.  Jay had already discovered
that he was not born to be a farmer—by a large
majority.

The next morning the ambitious youth hastily rose
from the breakfast-table, held out his hand to his surprised father, and said " Good-by."  There were tears,
entreaties, warnings, but he burst away, seized his
little bundle of clothes, and started afoot through the
wild and sparsely-settled regions over the mountains
to Hobart Academy, with 50 cents in his pocket.
Thirty-two years later, being charged with treacher-
ously selling out his associates, he laid upon a table

stocks and bonds of his own of the value of $35,000,-000.

Arrived at Hobart, and canvassing the town for work, he got a chance to keep books for the village blacksmith, who had started a little store next to the shop. This helped him out. He spent mornings and evenings with the son of Vulcan and paid his way at school. He rested little, played little, talked little, worked hard, like Napoleon at the artillery school at Brienne. He made surprising progress. In six months he had learned what the academy had to teach and left it. He left the village blacksmith too, and entered a hardware store as clerk, devoting his evenings to a systematic study of trigonometry and surveying. He rose at 4 in the morning and gave three hours to book and slate. He borrowed an old compass and a set of surveying tools, and, inducing the boys of the village to become his flag and chain bearers by presenting to them toys of his own manufacture, he succeeded in learning practical surveying " without a master."

At the same time he applied himself to the hardware business so energetically that at the age of 15 the little prodigy was made full partner and intrusted with the entire charge of the business. He came to New York for the first time in his life, and was able to open accounts with Phelps, Dodge & Co., and other heavy houses. But he had not yet found his career. The hardware trade was not congenial, and the same year, 1852, he slipped out, left his little capital behind, put his father in his place, and engaged to take charge of a surveying party at $20 a month, to complete the map of Ulster County. He organized his party, and started with five dollars in his pocket; walked 40 miles the first day, and worked a fortnight, when his employer suddenly "failed" before he had paid them a cent. Gould at once resolved to carry out the survey himself. What now happened to the 15-year old boy is best told in Mr. Gould's own words:

"I was out of money, that is to say, all I had was a 10-cent piece, and with that last coin I determined not to part. (I did not part with it and never shall; I keep it now as a memento.) Fall was approaching, and unless our surveys were finished before winter set in they would be postponed until the next spring, subjecting us to additional expense, and perhaps causing their abandonment. I determined to go ahead if possible. But how? I had neither time nor money to go back to Delaware County for supplies. I was among entire strangers and without credit. I could neither advance nor retreat without money, and so deeply did I deplore the ruin of our project that I shed tears.

"Tired out by my last day's tramp, hungry, and dejected, I was resting in a rocky nook near the town of Shawaugunk, my tears trickling down on the face of the compass, when I was suddenly hailed by a farmer, who asked me to go home with him and make a noon-mark—a north and south line so drawn that the shadow of an upright object falling upon it will indicate midday. I was asked to take dinner first, and joyfully accepted, as I had supped on two small crackers the previous night, and had been hard at work since daylight, and felt exceedingly faint. After a hearty dinner I made the noon-mark, and was about to bid the hospitable farmer good-by, when he asked what I charged for the work. I said I charged nothing—he was welcome to it; but he offered me half a dollar, insisting that it was the price a neighbor had paid for one. I accepted the money and departed rejoicing. If I had discovered a new continent I would not have been more elated, for, with 60 cents in my pocket and the prospect of making other noon-marks along the route, I saw a way to carry my enterprise through. I can never forget that day. From that time forward the fame of my noon-marks preceded me. Applications came in from the farmers all around, and out of this new source of supply I paid all the expenses of my surveys and came out at the completion with $6 in my pocket."

A respectable sum was received from the map. Young Gould now became a professional surveyor and civil engineer. He mapped Albany, Ulster, Greene, and Delaware Counties, in New York, Lake and Geauga Counties in Ohio, and Oakland County in Michigan; made the surveys for a plank road and a railroad; wrote and published a history of Delaware County; started a tannery, where he employed 250 men; built a town (Gouldsboro); and established a bank, and carried it through the panic of 1857, before he was 21.

He sold an interest in his town for $80,000, and invested the money in depreciated railroad securities after the panic. Soon after this he secured a controlling interest in two railroads, and it was not long before he embarked all his fortunes in the Erie, with what success is well known. With herculean energy he has reached out and gathered in the reins of transportation dropped by other hands, till now he is the central figure of 30,000 miles of railroad communication, and the most potent financial genius in the Republic.

His present quarrel with the Mutual Union Tele-graph, undertaken in behalf of his pet, the Western Union, is said to worry Mr. Gould more than any-thing else he has recently done. He is surprised to see the new company develop such fighting qualities, and he has been tempted to do some things of the Jim Fisk order that are not regarded as quite square by his associates, Cyrus Field, Dr. Green, Gen. Eck-ert, and men sensitive to business honor—such as the recent breaking open and examining of John G. Moore's private papers during his absence from the city.

Jay Gould is not " nice," but his quarrels do not rankle. Russel Sage said to me a fortnight ago: " Gould is one of the best-natured of men. After the failure of that persistent conspiracy to ruin him, in which his fingers certainly were pinched some, he was just as pleasant as ever with the parties to it; he dealt with them as freely as ever, and gave them as many chances as anybody. But while the contest lasts he never lets up. The bears at present are not having a very good time in their dealings with him."

Mr. Gould lives in an unpretentious but spacious mansion at the corner of Fifth avenue and Forty-sec-ond street in the winter time. His tastes are simple and democratic. His habits are thoroughly domestic.

He is not likely to die as Tom Scott died three years
ago ; for he uses neither liquor nor tobacco, loves his
family, retires at 10 and rises at 6.   Mr. Gould has a
fine library, with a choice selection of books, strong
in the department of history, and he is a close student
out of business hours.   He is not a religious man, like
Russel Sage, but goes to church sometimes.

Mrs. Gould is a daughter of a Mr. Miller, a retired
grocer of the city, and is a quiet, refined and interesting lady.   There are six children, equally divided between the sexes, and the three boys are all in business
with their father.   The eldest, George J. Gould, a
youth of 22, is a member of the firm of W. E. Connor & Co., of which Mr. Morsini is also a member,
and Jay Gould himself is special partner.   Connor,
by the way, known to his familiars as " Wash," began
life as Mr. Gould's office-boy, and is now a millionaire—and more, too.

The Gould summer-house is at " Lyndhurst," near
Irvington, up the Hudson, and comprises about 600
acres of beautiful land, and one of the finest conser-
vatories and graperies in America.   Rare plants and
flowers have been sent to him from all parts of the
world, until his place is stocked with the choice plants
of every zone and meridian.   Mr. Gould has made a
close study of botany, and can call most of his plants

by name.  He has now in his gallery hundreds of valuable paintings, his own taste running to modern art —the best works of the French masters—Meissonier, Millet, Delaroche, Bouguereau, Delacroix, etc.

In his office he is very reserved and laconic.  His associates and clerks have learned to read his meaning from a word or look.  His mail is encumbered every day with scores of begging letters, which never reach him, but are destroyed by his secretary.  He agrees with Russel Sage and other wealthy men that promiscuous charity is to be avoided, and he gives only to the best attested cases.  During the yellow fever troubles he telegraphed to the Mayor of Memphis, " Draw on me for all the money you want."

Mr. Gould seldom goes to balls ; doesn't care for general society ; avoids display , never reads novels ; spends most of his spare time in  the large room that is walled up with 5,000 volumes of standard literature of a solid sort.

# THURLOW WEED

—

FIFTY YEARS A JOURNALIST.

Thurlow Weed, the Nestor of American journalists, was born on November 15, 1797, at Catskill, Greene County, N. Y., whither his parents had emigrated from Stamford, Conn., in the hopes of bettering their slender fortunes. Joel Weed, his father, was a worthy honest, industrious carman, who, despite his best efforts, was often in jail for debt, and among the earliest boyish recollections of young Thurlow were his visits to his father when in confinement, or " on the limits." The boy, by the way, was originally named Edward Thurlow, after Edward Lord Thurlow, Chancellor of the Realm, but the Edward was soon dropped. There was little or no schooling for the children of the poor in the early days of the Republic, and young Thurlow at an early age was helping to earn money to support the family. He found occasional employment in running errands and doing odd jobs, and when about 10

THURLOW WEED.

years of age began to shift for himself. He became first a cabin-boy and then a deck hand on board the sloop Jefferson, and afterwards on the sloop Ranger. He spent an entire summer in this way, earning a few dollars a month, which were cheerfully sent home. After a year's cruising he abandoned the water, owing to attacks of vertigo whenever he attempted to mount the rigging. During his seaman life he first visited New York, and while there he earned his first shilling by carrying the trunk of one of the sloop passengers up Broad street to a hotel. In the winter of 1808 Joel Weed moved his family further west, to Cincinnatus, Cortland County, N. Y. Young Thurlow went to work with a will at the new avocations before him, helping in the asheries, the tanneries, the logging, the fencing, the clearing, the plowing, and the other duties pertaining to farm life in that section. While here, Weed enjoyed the advantage of a few months' schooling in the rudiments at a little country schoolhouse, and improved every opportunity to satisfy his growing passion for reading. In the winter of 1811 he attained the height of his boyish ambition when his proffered services were accepted as an apprentice in the office of a small weekly newspaper called the *Lynx*, published by Theodore C. Fay, at Onondaga Hollow, Onondaga County, N. Y. At first the tall, strong awk-

ward boy was assigned to the laborious task of " tread-
ing pelts " and pulling at the old Ramage press. But he
soon rose from apprentice to journeyman, and trudg-
ing on foot from town to town obtained employment
in one printing-office after another. Among the
various places at which he worked at the case or at
the press were Onondaga Hollow, Manlius, Auburn,
Geneva, Albany, New York, Herkimer, and Cooperstown. During the war of 1812, young Weed was in
the army, having enlisted in a Herkimer County regiment under Col. Petrie, in 1813. He was shortly
after made Quartermaster-Sergeant, and spent several
months in camp life at Sackett's Harbor, N. Y. After
the war he was employed in various offices in Franklin
Square and Pearl Street, in New York, at one time being a fellow-workman with James Harper, the late
head of the great publishing house. Mr. Weed was
an excellent, industrious workman, whose dissipations
were confined to the theater—he was passionately
fond of the drama—and a stroll upon the Battery, the
then fashionable resort. Here he became acquainted
by sight with the leading personages of the metro-
polis, and soon came to know the men who played a
prominent part in political life. He had a natural
proclivity toward politics, as he had toward the printing office. He was an active worker at local meet-

ings and at the polls on election days, although deprived himself of the right of suffrage on account of the property qualification for voters. In April, 1818, Mr. Weed married Miss Catherine M. Ostrander, of Cooperstown, N. Y., a woman of remarkably good sense and prudence, industry, religious principles, and domestic habits, whose thrift did much to build up a competence out of her husband's slender income.

His marriage led Mr. Weed to look for higher and more remunerative employment. He now aspired to be an editor. His first connection with the press as an editor was in Chenango County, where he started the weekly *Republican Agriculturist*, in December, 1818. It was Clintonian in politics, and supported the project of constructing the Erie Canal. In 1821, he purchased an interest in the Manlius *Times*, which he sold out a year or two later. Going to Rochester he secured the position of assistant editor on the Rochester *Telegraph*. The entire control of the paper was soon left in his hands, and by his tact and address in political writing and management he rose rapidly in the esteem of the citizens of that town, so that when Rochester felt the need of a bank, Mr. Weed was unanimously chosen to go to Albany to get the necessary charter. His mission was so satisfactory that in 1824 Rochester sent him to the State Assembly. During his single year's service in the Legislature he displayed the skill for political manipulation, which characterized his after-life. It is claimed that through his management the legislative caucus, which was expected to choose Electors favorably to Gen. Jackson under party pressure, were supplied with a mixed ticket, enabling them to follow their own inclinations, and chose Electors whose votes were cast as follows: Adams, 26 ; Crawford, 5 ; Clay, 4 ; Jackson, 1. Returning to Rochester he became editor and half owner of the *Telegraph*, whose circulation and influence was steadily increasing. The mysterious disappearance of Capt. William Morgan and the anti-Masonic craze which followed the alleged Masonic murder suddenly became important factors in Mr. Weed's life. He took the anti-Masonic side, and in the hight of the excitement the *Telegraph* went went down through the withdrawal of all Masonic support.

The anti-Masonic party soon began not only to nominate, but elect public officers in the western part of the State. Their success then filled them with hopes of political ascendancy in the State and perhaps in the Nation. One of the first needs of the new party was an organ at the State Capital, where it had already had a respectable representation in the Legislature. By general consent Thurlow Weed was chosen to conduct this paper. The necessary fund as easily raised, and on March 22, 1830, the first number of the Albany *Evening Journal* appeared. Before the Spring was over the paper was acknowledged to be *the* organ of the Anti-Masonic party. At that time Mr. Weed constituted the staff of the paper. He was editor-in-chief, managing editor, news editor, local reporter, legislative reporter, and proof reader. This work occupied his days. His evenings were spent in political consultations.

The panic of 1837, growing out of the financial and commercial policy of Jackson and Van Buren, as was claimed, gave the Whigs the wished-for opportunity of overthrowing the Regency and securing control of New York. In 1838, Seward and Bradish, the Whig candidates, were elected Governor and Lieutenant-Governor, and the Whigs had a majority in the State Assembly. As the party gained in power and prestige, Mr. Weed found the field of his labors vastly enlarged. Formerly he had been organizing and building up a minority party, now he was the acknowledged leader of a party in control of the State Government and marching steadily on to the control of National affairs. So accustomed had the party grown to rely on the guidance of the *Evening Journal* and its editor that the politicians of the State were in constant consultation with Mr. Weed, who was already called " the Dictator," " the Warwick," " the Old Man," etc.

It is doubtful if any one man ever had such complete control of a party or had his advice so implicitly followed by its members as Mr. Weed in his relations to the Whig party.

The great secret of his sway undoubtedly was his disinterestedness. He sought no office for himself and would take none. Among the qualities which peculiarly marked Mr. Weed's career was his penetration of character displayed in his admirable selection of the right men for the right places. In 1838 the Whig Central Committee desiring to publish a campaign political paper, Mr. Weed went to New York in seach of an editor and returned with Horace Greeley, who edited the *Jeffersonian* in that campaign and the *Log Cabin* in the Presidential contest of 1840.

Mr. Weed was a thorough journalist and a " practical politician," of unerring memory, proverbial tact, miraculous intuitions, and great mastery over men. He preferred to be the power behind the throne rather than the semblance of power on the throne. He was repeatedly urged to run for offices, ranging from Vice-President down to Mayor of Albany, but invariably declined. Three times he was offered the English Mission by three different Presidents whom he had helped elect. Mr. Weed took a prominent part in the Harrisburg Convention and urged the selection of Gen. Harrison, in opposition to the desires of Henry Clay's friends. The popular whirlwind of " hard cider and log cabin" times which swept the country for "Tippecanoe and Tyler too " proved the wisdom of the choice. Mr. Weed's suggestion in regard to Cabinet officers and other prominent appointments were listened to with favor by Gen. Harrison, who made Francis Granger, of New York, his Postmaster-General, and would doubtless have dispensed the Federal patronage in New York, largely according to Mr. Weed's desires. But the Whig triumph was short-lived, as President Harrison died a few weeks after his inauguration.

In 1843, Mr. Weed made his first trip to Europe, remaining abroad some months and describing his travels in letters to the *Journal*, which were widely copied. The year 1851, brought to Mr. Weed a sad domestic affliction in the death of his only son. He went to Europe again early in the Winter, spending several months abroad in general travel.

The first Republican National Convention at Philadelphia, in 1856, when Senator Seward was suggested

on all sides as the proper candidate, Mr. Weed, un-
willing to risk a defeat of his favorite at such a time,
induced the New York delegation to go for Gen. Fremont, and act which led to his nomination. The success of the Republicans in New York was instantan-
eous. Gen. Fremont had 80,000 majority in the State.
John A. King was elected Governor, and the party
controlled the Legislature. Weed's first choice for
President was his best and life-long friend, William
H Seward. To put him in at the head of the Chicago
ticket he devoted all his extraordinary abilities. The
Republicans of New York were a unit for their " favorite
son," and so well were all the plans laid that Mr.
Weed did not consider defeat a possibility. Yet
speaking of the actual result, a short time since, he
said it seemed to him like a special stroke of Providence for the good of the United States. When the
balloting commenced on the third day of the convention Seward's friends were disappointed to find Pennsylvania, where Seward was strong, and where Cameron had led Seward's friends to expect his support,
going against him. The subsequent change of Pennsylvania from Cameron to Lincoln carried the nomination of the "Rail-Splitter" on the third ballot.
Mr. Weed, it is needless to say, was greatly disappointed at the defeat of Seward. Immediately after

the nomination, while annoyed and dejected, and about to leave Chicago, David Davis and Leonard Swett, who had worked zealously for Lincoln, came to Mr. Weed's room to converse with him about the approaching canvass. He frankly informed them that he was so greatly disappointed at the action of the convention that he was unable to talk or think on the subject, and was going to Iowa for a few days. At their request he stopped at Springfield on his way home and had an interview with Lincoln. Of this meeting Mr. Weed afterward wrote: " I had met Lincoln in the fall of 1848, when he took the stump in New England. He displayed throughout the conversation so much good sense, intuitive knowledge of human nature, and such familiarity with the virtues and infirmities of politicians, that I became impressed very favorably with his fitness for the duties which he was not unlikely to be called upon to discharge. The conversation lasted five hours, and when the train arrived on which we were to depart I was all the better prepared to go to work with a will in favor of Mr. Lincoln's election, as the interview had inspired me with confidence in his capacity and integrity." Directly after the convention the *Journal* did not place the Chicago ticket at the head of its editorial columns.

When the result of the Presidential contest was

known Mr. Weed was pressed to visit Mr. Lincoln
for the purpose of advising him on the formation of
the Cabinet.   At this meeting he first learned what
inducement had swayed the Pennsylvania delegation
to vote against Seward.   There were a number of
leading Republicans present, and, after discussion, all
the Cabinet positions were agreed on except that of
Secretary of the Treasury.   Nothing being said about
the place, Mr. Weed asked who was to have that department, and was surprised to hear that it was reserved for Simon Cameron.   Some objections to this
designation being made, the slate was revised, and
Cameron was put down for the War Department.
Between the President and Mr. Weed a strong attach-
ment grew up, and at various critical junctures in the
struggle the President entrusted the journalist with
missions of the most delicate and important nature.
Just before the outbreak of the War one of the duties
intrusted to him was to secure the influence of the
New York *Herald* on the side of the administration.
The sympathies of that paper were with the South;
and its opposition to Lincoln encouraged the Rebellion and strengthened the Rebel cause.   With its large
circulation in Europe the *Herald* was creating a dangerous public sentiment abroad, and the necessity of

securing a change of policy, was considered at a Cabinet meeting, at which it was decided that Mr. Weed
should be asked to undertake the task. Although he
and Mr. Bennett had not spoken to one another for
thirty years, Mr. Weed at the urgent request of President Lincoln sent word that he wished to see Mr.
Bennett, and was invited to visit him at Washington
Heights.

The two editors sat long at table, and, although
nothing was said directly about the policy of the *Herald*, Mr. Weed put the situation so forcibly, appealing
to Mr. Bennett's judgment and to his sense of duty,
as an influential journalist, to the Government and
the Union, that the *Herald* came out the next day as
a strong Union paper. Shortly after this episode Mr.
Weed's mission to England and France was undertaken. It was deemed important by Mr. Lincoln that
some gentleman of experience and intelligence, pos-
sessing a thorough knowledge of all the circumstances
which preceded and occasioned the Rebellion, should
be sent abroad to disabuse the public mind of false
impressions, especially in England and France, where
numerous agents of secession had been at work in
quarters too ready to accept versions of the existing
dispute unfavorable to the North. Mr. Weed was in-

duced to accept this task, and set sail with Archbishop Hughes as a fellow Commissioner in the Africa, on Nov. 6, 1861.

The news of the taking of Mason and Slidell was brought to Europe by the steamer which followed the Africa on which Mr. Weed and the Archbishop sailed. The feeling in England and France, as well as in this country, was such that the danger of war was most imminent. Antecedents and traditions led us to hope for sympathy in France, and to apprehend hostility in England. But with the exception of the Prince Napoleon, who, as Mr. Weed relates, was friendly to us, the French were opposed, at this time, to the Union. The Trent affair occurring as it did at a most critical moment, united "all England" for war. It was felt that unless the Confederate Commissioners, Mason and Slidell, were released, that war was inevitable. While matters stood in this uncertain shape Mr. Weed met Mr. McCullogh Torrens in London the next morning after his arrival, early in December, 1861. The introduction was at the hands of Mr. Peabody, the eminent philanthropist, who was an old friend of Mr. Weed's. Mr. Torrens said that the arrival of Mr. Weed was most opportune. He must see Earl Russell immediately. Mr. Weed replied that Mr. Adams, then our Minister, would present him to the

Earl as soon as practicable. " That will not do," said
Mr. Torrens. " Time presses, you must see the Earl
to-morrow," adding that he would arrange an audience
and let Mr. Weed know the time and place that evening. Mr. Weed was surprised at the warm interest
manifested by an Englishman and a stranger, and
doubtful as to the propriety of anticipating the kind
intentions of Mr. Adams, but that gentleman relieved
his doubt and advised him by all means to avail himself of this timely offer. Mr. Weed dined that day
with Sir J. Emerson Tennent, meeting a large and
what proved to be a war party of gentlemen, among
them the Colonel of a regiment which was to leave
London the next morning to embark at Liverpool for
Canada. The Colonel was toasted, and in response
made a brief but exciting war speech, dwelling with
much effect upon the duty of Englishmen to resent
the insult to their flag. Mr. Weed was seated at the
table next to Lord Paget, of the Admiralty, who informed him that their preparations for war were active
and formidable, and that for the first time since 1815
they were working " double-handed " night and day
in the dock-yards. In passing by the famous London
Tower Mr. Weed had himself heard that day the
clanking of arms that were in process of shipment for
instant service. Returning to his hotel after dinner

he found Mr. Torrens, who directed him to leave the
city the next morning at 11 o'clock, and drive to Pem-
broke Lodge, Earl Russell's country seat. Mr. Weed
found the Minister the next day alone, and was courteously received. Conversation was at first embar-
rassed by an evident determination on Earl Russell's
part to ignore all other questions until the honor of
England should be satisfied by the surrender of Mason
and Slidell. Gradually, however, the restraint passed
away, and his Lordship explained the circumstances
which led to the Queen's proclamation giving bellig-
erent rights to the Rebel States. He had come to the
conclusion that the North was the real aggressor.
After an hour and a half's conversation, during which
Mr. Weed endeavored to remove that impression,
lunch was announced, and the conversation became
general. In the drawing-room, after the Earl had
conversed aside with Lady Russell for a few minutes,
Mr. Weed was about to take leave, when Lady Russell interrupted, saying: "You must not go without
seeing the Lodge grounds," in walking through which
her Ladyship pointed out various objects with which
history had made her visitor familiar. In the course
of the walk she remarked that ladies, of course, knew
nothing of State secrets, but that they had ears, and
sometimes heard things not perhaps intended for

them, adding that it would probably relieve Mr.
Weed's anxiety to know that in our difficulties the
sympathies of the Queen were with the United States;
that her Majesty remembered the attentions extended
to her son, the Prince of Wales, and would do everything in her power to prevent a rupture with America.
With this gleam of hope Mr. Weed returned to his
hotel well satisfied with his visit to the Minister.

While waiting with the most intense solicitude for
the decision of our Government upon the demand for
the surrender of the Confederate Commissioners, Mr.
Weed received from his friend, the Hon. Arthur Kin-
naird, M. P., in the strictest confidence positive evidence that the Queen had at the right moment caused
the dispatch demanding the surrender of Mason and
Slidell to be so modified as to render a compliance
with it less difficult to Mr. Lincoln. Several days
after receiving this information, confirming the assurance of Lady Russell, Mr. Weed received additional
evidence from another high source, the honored and
lamented Sir Henry Holland, physician to the Queen,
who was a daily visitor at Mr. Weed's lodgings, and
often afterward, on his visits to New York, was a welcome guest at Mr. Weed's residence. Sir Henry had
been informed by the Queen what occurred between
her Majesty, Lord Palmerston, and Prince Albert,

when the dispatch demanding the surrender was brought to Windsor for approval. Whatever passes between the Queen and her Ministers, while a question is under consideration, is in its nature confidential, and Mr. Weed never felt that he was at liberty to make a full revelation of the facts within his knowledge, except to a few friends and members of his family. It is enough, perhaps, to know that on three occasions during the first year of the Rebellion her Majesty contributed essentially to the preservation of peace between this country and England, and that on two occasions she discountenanced suggestions from the French Government which meant war. When the consultation at Windsor Castle above referred to took place the Prince Consort, at the Queen's suggestion, made certain interlineations in the dispatch to Mr. Seward, which was, so Sir Henry informed Mr. Weed, "the last time that the Prince used his pen." The conflict between the Rebels and the Government at Washington was formidable enough, as we all realize now, without the aggravations of a simultaneous conflict with England and France. The French Emperor was unquestionably in favor of the Southern States, and desired to aid them even at the expense of a war with our Government. As soon as the tempest in England began to subside, Mr. Weed hastened to

Paris, with Gen. Winfield Scott as a fellow-passenger
On the way the thought occurred to him that a bold,
frank letter on the American question, signed by the
General, would have great weight. As soon as they
reached Paris the letter was prepared and published
at once in all the leading French and English newspapers.

From Prince Napoleon Mr. Weed received attention. The Prince, differing widely and boldly from
the Emperor, was the warm friend of our Government,
and sought to serve us. Mr. Weed was instant in season and out of season in explaining and defending the
cause of his country, and it was largely due to his
skillful and indefatigable efforts that the attempt to
unite France and England against the cause of the
Union failed. He induced the Emperor to alter a
paragraph in his speech to the French National Legislature in January, 1862, so that instead of expressing
a bitter opposition to the Union, as he had intended,
he spoke of it in a friendly tone. Prince Napoleon
was out of favor with " the nephew of his uncle " because of his pronounced sympathy for the North;
accordingly Mr. Weed worked upon the Emperor
through Prince de Morny, his brother.

The Prince de Morny based his opposition to the
Union cause largely, if not entirely, on the fact that

Charleston Harbor was obstructed. He denounced the obstruction as an outrage without precedent, which wrought great injury to the commercial interests of France, since it interrupted the exports of cotton to that country. Mr. Weed, when the Prince had finished his protest, proceeded to turn the tables on him by quoting from the treaty of Utrecht, which provided that the fortification of the city of Dunkirk should be razed, the harbor filled up, and the sluices which served to cleanse it leveled, and this, too, at the French King's expense! In the account which he subsequently gave of his *coup d'état*, Mr. Weed wrote of the effect of his reference to the treaty of Dunkirk as follows: "When the Count had read the article over twice very attentively I observed that he would find by referring to the history of that day that Holland, an ally of England in the war which ended with this treaty, complained two years afterward that its terms had not been complied with, inasmuch as the fortification and harbor had been but partially destroyed, while the article referred to called for their entire demolition. Yet Dunkirk at this day, instead of being (what it would have been but for the treaty of Utrecht) a large and prosperous commercial city, is wholly unused as a harbor, and utterly insignificant as a town. De Morny, after a pause, remarked that he was to accompany the Minister of Foreign Affairs (M. Thouvenel) to the Tuileries on the following evening, when the Emperor's speech would be read to them. . . . When the Emperor's speech was printed the passage relating to America was an amicable instead of a hostile one." The value of the services to the Union cause which Mr. Weed rendered in this connection can not be too highly estimated.

On his return from Europe in 1862 the gratitude of New York for what he had done for his country took the shape of a formal presentation to him of the freedom of the city, and several of his more intimate friends united in presenting him with a costly memorial in silver, which is one of the most precious heirlooms in the family.

In January, 1863, Mr. Weed dissolved his connection with the Albany *Journal*, both as editor and proprietor. In his valedictory, which appears in the issue for January 28, he frankly stated the reason which induced him to take the step. "We have fallen in evil times," he said. "Our country is in immediate and imminent danger. I differ widely with my party about the best means of crushing the Rebellion. The difference is radical and irreconcilable. I can neither impress others with my views nor surrender my own solemn convictions. The alternative of living in

strife with those whom I have esteemed or withdrawing is presented. I have not hesitated in choosing the
path of peace as the path of duty. If those who differ from me are right, and the country is safely carried
through its present struggle, all will be well and nobody hurt. . . . But for an infirm leg and a
broken arm, I would go into the army, for the country
is entitled to the service of all its citizens; and it is
more a privilege than a duty to defend a Government
under whose beneficent sway and benign rule we haye
enjoyed protection, prosperity and happiness, and in
the destruction of which the best hopes of the highest
civilization perish."

Since the close of the war Mr. Weed has lived in
retirement in New York, but has maintained a lively
interest in all public questions, and has frequently fa-
vored the metropolitan press with his views on the
topics of the day, and with reminiscenses. In 1872
he returned to active politics for a brief time, and
showed that his name had not lost its old-time cunning by springing the name of Gen. John A. Dix on
the Republican State Convention and securing his
nomination for Governor by a skillfully planned stam-
pede. The wisdom of his selection was demonstrated
by the triumphant election of the whole Republican
ticket. On March 22, 1880, he once more assumed

the editorship of the *Journal*—for one day—on the occasion of the celebration of the fiftieth anniversary of its foundation. He leaves three daughters, Mrs. William Barnes, of Albany, N. Y.; Mrs. James Alden, of Morrisania, N. Y.; and Miss Harriet Weed, who has been his constant companion since the death of his wife, about thirty years ago. He leaves an estate estimated at over one million of dollars.

# RULES FOR BEHAVIOR.

# RULES FOR BEHAVIOR.

---

## *ETIQUETTE.*

ETIQUETTE is, in point of fact, nothing more nor less than the law, written and unwritten, which regulates the society of civilized people, distinguishing them from the communities of barbarous tribes, whose lives are hard and their manners still harder. It is to a well disciplined and refined mind the fundamental principle of action in all intercourse with society, and they are interested in maintaining it in its integrity, and bound to heed and obey its simplest as well as more formal precepts.

Etiquette, like every other human institution, is of course liable to abuse; it may be transformed from a convenient and wholesome means of producing universal comfort into an inconvenient and burdensome restraint upon freedom and ease.

Etiquette, to be perfect, must be like a perfectly fitting garment, which, beautifying and adorning the person, mast yet never cramp or restrain perfect freedom of movement.

Most people have heard of the gentleman (?) who was perfect in his knowledge of the laws of etiquette, and who, seeing a man drowning, took off his coat and was about to plunge into the water to rescue him, when he suddenly remembered that he had never been introduced to the struggling victim, and resuming his coat, tranquilly proceeded upon his way. Too rigid an observance of the laws of etiquette makes them an absurdity and a nuisance.

Good breeding is, as Lord Chesterfield well says, "the result of much good sense, some good nature, and a little self-denial for the sake of others, and with a view to obtain the same indulgence from them."

Lord Bacon, in his admirable essay on Ceremonies, says: "Not to use ceremonies at all, is to teach others not to use them again, and so diminisheth respect to himself; especially they be not to be omitted to strangers and formal natures; but the dwelling upon them, and exalting them above the moon is not only tedious, but doth diminish the faith and credit of him that speaks.

To quote again from Lord Chesterfield, "Good

sense and good nature suggest civility in general; but in good breeding there are a thousand little delicacies which are established only by custom."

It is precisely these "little delicacies" which constitute the difference between politeness and etiquette. Politeness is that inborn regard for others which may dwell in the heart of the most ignorant boor, but etiquette is a code of outward laws which must be learned by the resident in good society, either from observation or the instruction of others.

It is a poor argument used against etiquette that it is not truthful, and that uncouth manners are more frank and sincere than polished and refined ones. Is truth then a hedgehog, always bristling and offensive. Cannot truth be spoken in courteous accents from a kind, gentle impulse, as well as blurted out rudely and giving pain and mortification? It is true that roughness and sincerity often abide together, but would it destroy the honesty to polish away the roughness?

True politeness must come from the heart, from an unselfish desire to please others and contribute to their happiness; when upon this natural impulse is placed the polish of a complete and thorough knowledge of the laws of etiquette, the manners must be perfect and graceful.

An English author says: " Etiquette may be defined

as the minor morality of life.   No observances, however minute, that tend to spare the feelings of others,
can be classed under the head of trivialities; and
politeness, which is but another name for general
amiability, will oil the creaking wheels of life more
effectually than any of those unguents supplied by
mere wealth or station."

" To be truly polite, one must be at once good, just
and generous," has been well said by a modern
French writer.

" True politeness is the outward visible sign of those
inward spiritual graces called modesty, unselfishness,
generosity.   The manners of a gentleman are the
index of his soul.   His speech is innocent, because
his life is pure; his thoughts are direct, because his
actions are upright; his bearing is gentle, because his
blood, and his impulses, and his training are gentle
also.   A true gentleman is entirely free from every
kind of pretence.   He avoids homage instead of ex
acting it.   Mere ceremonies have no attraction for
him.   He seeks not only to say civil things, but to do
them.   His hospitality, though hearty and sincere,
will be strictly regulated by his means.   His friends
will be chosen for their good qualities and good manners; his servants for their thoughtfulness and honesty;
his occupations for their usefulness, or their graceful-

ness, or their elevating tendencies, whether moral, or mental, or political. And so we come round again to our first maxims, *i. e.*, that 'good manners are the kindly fruit of a refined nature.' "

The most perfect law of politeness, the safest and surest guide in all that pertains to the true definition of a gentleman or lady is, after all, the Christian rule, " Do unto others as you would others should do unto you."

No one with this for a guide can ever fail in true, genuine politeness, and that politeness will soon lead him to learn and remember all the prevailing rules of established etiquette.

---

## INTRODUCTIONS.

NEVER introduce people to each other unless you are sure the acquaintance so commenced will be mutually agreeable.

When introducing two gentlemen, look first to the elder, or, if there is any difference in social standing, to the superior, and, with a slight bow, say to him: " Allow me to introduce my friend, Mr. Jones, to you;" then turning to your friend, repeat his name, and follow it by that of the gentleman to whom he is introduced, thus: " Mr. Smith, allow me to introduce

my friend, Mr. Jones, to you—Mr. Jones, Mr. Smith."
In introducing a gentleman to a lady, bow slightly to
the latter, saying, "Miss ——, allow me to introduce
Mr. ——; Mr. —— (bowing to him), Miss ——."

When several persons are introduced to one, it is
sufficient to name the single individual once, repeat-
ing all the names of the others thus: " Mr. Johnson,
allow me to introduce Mr. and Mrs. James, Miss
Smithson, Mr. Lewis, Mr. Johnson," bowing slightly
to each when named.

Shaking hands after an introduction has taken
place is merely optional, not necessary; and is forbidden to an unmarried lady to whom a gentleman is
introduced. A bow is all that etiquette requires. In
introducing young persons to elder ones of good social
standing, it is often a kindly act of encouragement
for the latter to shake hands, with a few cordial
words.

Should you, when walking with a friend, meet a lady
who desires to speak to you, your friend must stop
with you, yet an introduction under such circumstances
does not exact any future recognition.

If friends meet at public places of amusement and
are accompanied by strangers, introductions are not
required by etiquette, and if made do not oblige any
future acquaintance.

If at a dinner, a ball, or upon any occasion you are introduced, at a friend's house, to one with whom you are not on good terms, though it be your bitterest enemy, etiquette requires you to salute him or her courteously, and make no sign of resentment whilst under your friend's roof.

To introduce to a friend a person who is in any way objectionable, is an insult which fully justifies a withdrawal of friendship.

A gentleman should always raise his hat, if introduced in the street, to either lady or gentleman.

## LETTERS OF INTRODUCTION.

ETTERS of introduction should never be given, except to persons well known to the person introducing them, and addressed to those only who have a long-standing friendship for the writer.

Even amongst friends of long standing they should be given very cautiously and sparingly, as it is a great responsibility to send to your friend a visitor who may prove disagreeable, and you have no right whatever to call upon comparative strangers to extend hospitality or courtesy to your friends.

Letters of introduction should always be as short and concise as possible. If you wish to send any information to your friends about their visitor, send it in a separate letter by mail.

The utmost brevity is of importance in the letter of introduction, as it is usually read in the presence of the party introduced, and the pause must necessarily be awkward.

Letters of introduction must be left unsealed invariably; they should be folded and addressed like any other letter, but it is a gross breach of etiquette to prevent the bearer from reading what you may have said of him to your friend.

A letter of introduction should not be delivered in person. It should be sent, with the card of the person introduced, to the person to whom it is addressed, by a servant. The person receiving it should then call at once or send a written invitation to his house, and the person introduced may then call in person.

Letters of introduction soliciting favors should be but seldom given, and never unless the claims upon both parties interested are very strong.

Letters of introduction to and from business men, for business purposes, may be delivered by the bearers in person, and etiquette does not require the receiver to entertain the person introduced as the private friend of the writer.

Letters of introduction are very useful to travelers, or those about to change their place of residence; care, however, should be especially taken in the latter case to present persons to each other only, who will prove mutually agreeable, as it is surely no friendly act to force upon your friends a life-long acquaintance, perhaps with uncongenial persons.

In traveling abroad it is impossible to have too many letters of introduction. They take up but little room in a trunk, but their value when you find yourself "a stranger in a strange land," cannot be over-estimated.

## SALUTES AND SALUTATIONS.

MEN in this country acknowledge an introduction by extending the right hand in greeting —the whole hand—for it is positively insulting to offer two fingers, as some under-bred snobs will sometimes do, and it is almost as bad to extend the left hand, unless two persons are introduced at the same time, or the right hand is useless or occupied; in any such case apologize for the hand extended.

In offering the hand to a friend in the house, always

remove the glove, and grasp the hand given in return firmly for a moment. In the street, however, the glove may be retain ed, if it would cause an awkward pause to remove it; but always in such a case apologize for the covered hand.

In shaking hands, do not try to wring them off the wrists, nor press them as in a vise, nor pull them as though they were bell-handles, nor fling the two together with violence, so as to cause a report. Let the palms grasp each other firmly, but without any display of energy, and shake the hand moderately for a moment, then release it.

If a gentleman meet a gentleman, he may salute him by touching his hat without removing it, but if a lady be with either gentleman, both hats must be lifted in salutation.

A gentleman may bow to a lady seated at a window, if he is passing on the street, but he must not bow from a window to a lady on the street.

A gentleman may never offer to shake hands with a lady, but he must accept such an offer on her part, taking her hand lightly but firmly in his ungloved right one, and delicately shaking it for a moment.

In entering a church, a gentleman must remove his hat as soon as his foot crosses the threshold of the sacred edifice.

A gentleman may always bow to a lady he may meet on a stairway, even if not acquainted. If at the foot of the stairs, he must bow, pass her and ascend before her. If at the head of the stairs, he must bow, and wait for her to precede him in the descent.

In entering a room, a gentleman must take his hat, cane and gloves in his left hand, leaving his right hand free for salutation.

If a gentleman, walking with a friend, meets a lady with whom his friend is acquainted, he must also bow, although the lady may be a stranger to him.

A gentleman must always return a bow made to him in the street, even if he fails to recognize the person who makes it. It may be a person to whom he has been introduced, but whose face he has forgotten, and if it is an error on the part of the other, a courteous return of the salute will greatly diminish the embarrassment of the mistaken party.

In meeting a party of friends, with some of whom you are intimately acquainted, and with some only slightly, endeavor to make your salutations as equal as possible.

In meeting at a friend's house, where you are visiting, a circle who are all entire strangers to you, remember that as mutual friends of the host and hostess you are bound, whilst under the same roof, to consider

yourselves as acquaintances.   No spirit of exclusive
ness is an apology for a neglect of this, and no shy.
ness can excuse a withdrawing into a corner, oı
clinging to one friend alone in such a circle.

––––––

## CALLS.

GENTLEMEN in society may make morning
calls upon all the following occasions :

In answer to a letter of introduction sent to
him, or to return the call if the letter is personally
presented.

In return for any hospitality offered to him when
visiting another city, if the entertainer visit his own
place of abode.

On any occasion when a grief or a joy calls for expressions of condolence or congratulation in the circle
of his friends.

To greet the safe return of any friend who has been
abroad, or away from home for any length of time.

Following any occasion when a lady has accepted
his services as an escort, a gentleman must call to in--
quire after the health of his fair charge, and must not
delay longer than the day after that upon which he
has escorted the lady.

After a wedding, at the time appointed for the reception of friends.

When visiting in another city, upon any friends there, or upon those to whom letters of introduction have been given.

In asking or granting a favor, a call is demanded by etiquette.

Morning calls must never be earlier than noon, evening ones never later than nine o'clock.

A gentleman may never call with a friend upon a lady, unless the friend is previously acquainted, or he has obtained permission of the lady to introduce him.

In making a formal call, a gentleman must retain his hat in his hand. An umbrella or cane may be left in the hall, never the hat or gloves. If the call is made in the evening, the hat and gloves must be held until the host or hostess gives an invitation to lay them aside and spend the evening. Strict etiquette requires that such an invitation shall not be given, or if given, not accepted on the occasion of a first call.

In making an informal call in the evening, a gentleman may leave hat, gloves, cane and overcoat in the hall.

No gentleman will prolong a call if he finds his host or hostess dressed to go out. A brief visit with a promise to repeat it will place his entertainers at ease.

A card used in calling must never have anything upon it, but the name and address of the caller. Nothing can show a greater ignorance of the customs of society than to use a business card for a friendly call. A physician may put the prefix Dr. or the professional M. D., upon his card, and an Army or Navy officer his rank and branch of service.

It is in bad taste for a caller to preface his or her departure by consulting a watch, remarking, " Now I must go," or insinuating that the hostess is weary of the visitor. Rise when ready to go, and express your pleasure at finding your friends at home, followed by a cordially expressed dcsire for a speedy meeting again.

Pelham said he always withdrew when he said something that produced a sensation, because he knew he must leave such an impression as would make people wish to see him again.

When other callers arrive, it is in bad taste to rise at once as if driven away. Let the first caller watch for a favorable opportunity to retire gracefully.

If a gentleman calling sees a lady unescorted rise to go, he may with perfect propriety offer to escort her to her carriage, even if a stranger, but he must return again to make his own farewell bow to the hostess.

If strangers are in the room when a caller rises to leave, courtesy requires only a slight bow in passing.

When calling, etiquette requires that a card be sent up. It will show that you have called, and if friends are at home, will prevent any confusion from mis pronunciation of your name by the servant.

When the lady of the house is not at home, a card must be left, and if there are two or more ladies, the turning down of one corner of the card signifies that the call was intended for all the family.

If cards to be left preparatory to leaving town, the initials p. p. c. (*pour prendre conge,** or, presents parting compliments), must be written in the left hand corner. If the departure is a hurried one, the card may be sent by a servant, but it is in better taste to leave it in person.

Visits of condolence are made within a week after the bereavement, unless the deceased be one of the immediate family, when a fortnight may be allowed to intervene.

The first call of a stranger must be returned within a week.

Married men are not obliged to make calls of cere-

* To take leave.

20

mony in person. It is sufficient for their wives to leave their cards with their own.

Residents in a place make the first call upon any new comers.

It is not necessary, nor is it customary in the city, to offer refreshments to callers. In the country, especially if the visitors have come from a distance, it is not only courteous, but often a positive kindness to do so.

If a stranger come to stay at the house of a friend, those who are in the habit of visiting at the house should call as soon as possible, and such calls should be returned at the earliest practicable opportunity.

A well-bred person should endeavor to be always prepared for callers. Illness alone, either your own, or that of some one requiring your constant attention, can only excuse you.

It is ill-bred to enter a drawing-room, with a handsome carpet upon it, in muddy boots and spattered garments, to stand a dripping umbrella beside you, or deposit over-shoes in the hall.

Never resume your seat after having once left it to say adieu. There is nothing more awkward than to take leave twice.

If you find yourself intruding upon an early dinner hour, do not prolong your stay.

It is a breach of etiquette, during a call, to draw near to the fire to warm your hands and feet, unless you are invited by the mistress of the house to do so. If you are alone in the drawing-room for a time, while your visit is announced, and then go to the fire, leave your seat and advance to meet the mistress of the house as she enters, and then take the seat she points out to you.

In visiting an invalid, never offer to go to the room, but wait for an invitation to do so.

A gentleman who is a confirmed invalid, may receive the visits of a lady friend, but under no other circumstances.

It is a breach of etiquette to remove the gloves when making a formal call.

It is a breach of etiquette for a caller, who is waiting the entrance of the hostess, to open the piano, or to touch it if it is open.

It is a breach of etiquette to walk round the room when waiting for your hostess, examining the furniture or pictures.

It is a breach of etiquette for a caller to open or shut a door, raise or lower a window curtain, or in any way alter the arrangement of a room.

It is a breach of etiquette to turn your chair so as to bring your back to any one seated near to you.

It is a breach of etiquette when making a call, to play with any ornament in the room, finger the furniture, or seem indeed to be aware of anything but the company present.

To prolong a call to the next meal time is a positive rudeness, as it forces your hostess to invite you to the table whether convenient and agreeable or not.

In calling upon friends at a boarding-house or a hotel, always write their names above your own upon your card, that it may be certain to be delivered to the right person.

## CONVERSATION.

THERE are several principal rules of etiquette which must be rigidly observed in conversation, the non-observance of which will at once stamp the guilty party as ignorant of the forms and customs of polite society.

The personal pronouns should be used as little as possible when speaking of any one, either present or absent. The name of the lady or gentleman to whom reference is made, should be repeated if necessary, but under no circumstances should the words "she" or "he," accompanied by a nod or jerk of the thumb, in the direction of the person spoken of, be employed.

Avoid as utterly hateful the use of slang terms. In a gentleman, such expressions are too suggestive of low company, and intercourse with the worst associates, and in a lady such expressions are too offensive to be tolerated at all in good society. Slang never ornamented conversation, but it invariably sullies and degrades it.

Never hold your companion, in a conversation, by the button-hole.

Do not interlard your conversation with scraps of foreign language. It is an affectation of knowledge in one direction, and a sort of tacit admission of ignorance in another; for it would seem to show that the speaker was not well enough acquainted with his own language to be able to express by its aid that which could really be told as well, perhaps better, by it than any other.

Quotations are to be avoided as much as possible. When made, they should be exceedingly short. Short, pungent, epigrammatic quotations, if suitable to the subject of conversation, may be occasionally introduced, but their use should be the exception, not the rule.

Dr. Johnson says that in order to converse well, "there must, in the first place, be knowledge—there must be materials; in the second place, there must be

a command of words; in the third place, there must
be imagination to place things in such views as they
are not commonly seen in; and in the fourth place,
there must be a presence of mind, and a resolution
that is not to be overcome by failure—this last is an
essential requisite; for want of it many people do not
excel in conversation."

To be known as an inveterate teller of stories, is a
great injury to a man in society.  A short, brilliant
anecdote, that is especially applicable to the conversation, known to be new and never printed, is all that a
well-bred man will ever permit himself to inflict.

Remarks having, and intended to have, a double
meaning—even puns—are utterly to be deprecated.

Political and religious topics are not in good taute
in general conversation.

To listen with interest and attention is as importaat
in polite society as to converse well, and it is in the
character of listener that the elegant refinement of a
man accustomed to society will soonest prove itself.

Avoid as much as possible all egotism; in conversation stick closely to Cardinal Wolsey's direction to
"love thyself last."  It is, to say the least of it, unseemly for a man to be constantly making himself the
subject of conversation.

There used to be a joke against Lord Erskine, who

was notably a talker of himself, that the printer, having to print a speech which his lordship had delivered, sent word to say that "he was very sorry, but he had no more 'I's' in his founts than would suffice to set up half the speech."

Suitable subjects, for time and place, form an important consideration in polite conversation. Grave tones and important consideration are not suited for the chit-chat of a brief call or a social evening, nor is small talk an appropriate introduction, when the meetings are for the purpose of discussing serious matters Let gayety or gravity rule as plaee and occasion demand.

Gesticulations are in excessively bad taste. If you do not wish to attract censorious remark, converse quietly and without gesture.

Refrain from the use of satire, even if you are master of the art. It is permissible only as a guard against impertinence, or for the purpose of checking personalities, or troublesome intrusions. It must never be employed by a gentleman against a lady, though ladies are prone to indulge in the use of this wordy weapon. Their acknowledged position should, in the eyes of a true gentleman, shield them from all shafts of satire. If they, on the other hand, choose to indulge in satire, it is the part of a gentleman to remonstrate gently, and if the invective be continued, to withdraw.

Do not attempt to speak with the mouth full.

Do not, however much you may be pleased with any remark, cry out "Bravo!" clap your hands, or permit any gesture, silent or otherwise, to mark your appreciation of it.

If you are flattered, repel it by quiet gravity. Refrain, too, from expressions of flattery to others; you will surely offend any hearer who has delicacy of feeling and refinement.

If an error in language, either in pronunciation or grammar, escapes those with whom you are conversing, never show that you notice it.

In addressing any one and in general conversation, it will be well to bear in mind the advice of Polonius to his son Laertes: "Be thou familiar, but by no means vulgar." In society, a man should make himself as agreeable as he can, doing his best to assist conversation, as well by talking gracefully and easily, as by listening patiently, even though it be to a twice-told tale.

Do not whistle, loll about, scratch your head, or fidget with any portion of your dress while speaking. 'Tis excessively awkward, and indicative of low-breeding

Strictly avoid anything approaching to absence or mind. Lord Chesterfield said: "When I see a man absent in mind, I choose to be absent in body." And there was really much reason in the remark.

Whispering is atrocious, and cannot be tolerated. Private affairs must be delayed for private interviews.

Unless you are actually afflicted with deafness, never ask to have a sentence repeated.

Never interrupt a speaker. It is equally rude to supply words over which your companion may hesitate a moment.

In general conversation avoid argument. If obliged to discuss a point, do so with suavity, contradicting, if necessary, with extreme courtesy, and if you see no prospect of agreement, finishing off with some happy, good-natured remark to prove that you are not hurt or offended.

When addressing a person, look in his or her face, not staringly, but frankly, never fixing your eyes on the carpet or your boots.

Loud laughing and giggling are in excessively bad taste.

Eschew scandal, for "in scandal as in robbery, the receiver is always thought as bad as the thief." Mimicry is the lowest and most ill-bred of all buffoonery.

Bashfulness is an inconvenient quality, which a grea authority has stated to be " the distinguishing charactei of a booby."

Nicknames are abominable, and are never allowed in good society.

If your friends become the subject of conversation, never compare one with another, or mention the vices of one to add to the lustre of virtue of the other.

Do not commence any conversation by the suggestion of painful or disagreeable topics. To ask a friend abruptly, " For whom are you in mourning ? " may be tearing open anew a wound that was covered for the time by intercourse with society.

Subjects or incidents calculated to disgust the hearers, are to be avoided in polite conversation.

Do not use surnames alone, even if speaking of intimate friends.

Let no more than one person be speaking at one time.

If you would preserve a character for truthfulness, avoid the too common fault of exaggeration.

Cant is simply detestable.

The talented author of " Good Society " says:

" The great secret of talking well is to adapt your conversation as skilfully as may be to your company. Some men make a point of talking commonplace to all ladies alike, as if a woman could only be a trifler. Others, on the contrary, seem to forget in what respects the education of a lady differs from that of a gentleman, and commit the opposite error of conversing on topics with which ladies are seldom acquainted. A woman of sense has as much right to be annoyed by the one, as a lady of ordinary education by the other. You cannot pay a finer compliment to a woman of refinement and *esprit*, than by leading the conversation into such a channel as may mark your appreciation of her superior attainments.

"It should be remembered that people take more interest in their own affairs than in anything else which you can name. In *tete a tete* conversations, therefore, lead a mother to talk of her children, a young lady of her last ball, an author of his forthcoming book, or an artist of his exhibition picture.

"Remember in conversation that a voice 'gentle and low' is, above all other extraneous accomplishments, an 'excellent thing in woman.' There is a certain distinct but subdued tone of voice which is peculiar to persons only of the best breeding. It is better to err by the use of too low than by too loud a tone. Loud laughter is extremely objectionable in society."

To invariably commence a conversation by remarks

on the weather, shows a poverty of ideas that is truly pitiable.

A person who has traveled will probably be severely ridiculed if constantly referring to "the winter I spent in Florence," or "when I was in London."

If conversation takes a tone that is offensive to good taste, charity or justice, be silent.

Be not too ready to correct any statement you may deem untrue. You máy be yourself mistaken.

When visiting, be careful that you do not appear to undervalue anything around you by comparing it with what you have at home.

--------

## STREET ETIQUETTE.

WHEN a gentleman recognizes a friend in the course of his walk, he must lift his hat with the hand farthest from him. Lifting the hat is a sufficient recognition between gentlemen; but in meeting a lady, an old gentleman, or a clergyman, it is necessary to bow also.

No gentleman may smoke when walking with a lady.

To eat anything, even confectionery, in the street, is a sign of low breeding.

If a gentleman wishes to shake hands with a friend, he must lift his hat with the left hand, leaving the right free to extend. Never must he give his left hand, or extend a portion of the right. The whole right hand is *en regle*.

If a gentleman is walking with a lady, he should insist upon carrying any book, parcel, or umbrella she may have with her.

Swinging the arms is an awkward and ill-bred habit.

To attempt to cross the street between the carriages of a funeral procession is rude and disrespectful; and we cannot but commend the foreign custom of removing the hat, and standing in a respectful attitude until the melancholy train has passed.

When a gentleman is walking alone, he must always turn aside to give the upper side of the pavement to a lady, to any one carrying a heavy load, to a clergyman, or to an old gentleman.

Never push violently through a crowd. If a gentleman or lady is really in haste, a few courteous words will open a passage more quickly than the most vigorous pushing or shoving.

If a gentleman and lady are obliged to cross a narrow walk, plank, or slippery place, the lady may go first, and the gentleman walk close behind her, to aid her it needful. If the place is short, then the gentleman should go first, and then offer his hand to assist the lady across. If a gentleman meet a lady or old gentleman at such a crossing, he may, with perfect propriety, assist them in crossing, even if perfect strangers to him.

A gentleman must hold his hat in his hand if he stops to inquire his own way, or to direct another.

If a gentleman sees a lady alone hesitating at a bad crossing, or leaving a carriage at an awkward place, he may offer his hand to assist her in crossing or alighting, raise his hat, bow, and pass on. A lady may, with perfect propriety, accept such assistance from a stranger, thanking him, and returning his bow.

If a lady leaves an omnibus or car alone, the gentleman nearest the door should alight, assist her out, and enter the omnibus again.

Gentlemen should always pass up the fare of ladies in an omnibus.

In a public conveyance, a gentleman should offer his seat to any lady who is standing.

Loud talking and laughing in the street are sure signs of vulgarity.

Never look back after any one passing; it is extremely ill-bred.

Staring is a mark of low breeding.

Whispering in a public conveyance is excessively rude.

Never call out loudly to an acquaintance who may be passing.

Young persons, meeting elderly friends in the street, should wait for a recognition before speaking, and then bow respectfully. To nod carelessly at an old person is rude, if not actually insulting.

If you meet two gentlemen in the street, and wish to speak to one of them, apologize to the other, and make the detention as brief as possible.

A gentleman walking with a lady, should endeavor to accommodate his steps to hers, not force her to stride along or trot with short steps for his long ones

Lounging over a counter is ill-bred.

Putting your elbows on a counter is rude.

Pushing aside another person is an act of ill-breeding.

A gentleman walking with two ladies may offer an arm to each of them, and they may thus sandwich him if they wish.

If a gentleman is walking with two ladies in a rain-storm, and there is but one umbrella, he should give it to his companions and walk outside. Nothing can be more absurd than to see a gentleman walking between two ladies holding an umbrella, which perfectly protects himself, and sends little streams of water from every point on the dresses of the ladies he is supposed to be sheltering.

It is in bad taste to talk of personal matters in the street, or to call loudly the names of persons you may mention. It is impossible to say who may be near to you. To discuss friends by name in a public conveyance of any kind is rude in the extreme.

If you meet a friend with whom you wish to shake hands, never put out your own until you are quite near, as nothing looks more awkward than hands extended to grasp each other two or three yards apart.

Never turn a corner at full speed, or you may find yourself knocked down or knocking down another by the violent contact.

Never talk politics or religion in a public conveyance.

Never stop to quarrel with a hack-driver. Pay his fare and dismiss him; if you have any complaint to make, take his number, and make it to the proper authorities. To keep a lady standing while you are disputing with a hack-man is extremely rude.

It is a sign of ill-breeding to change your seat in a car or omnibus. If you are unfortunate enough to have a neighbor who is positively annoying and unendurable, it is better to get out and take the next conveyance than to move to the other side. A gentleman may move from a crowded side to one left comparatively vacant.

---

## TRAVELING.

**T**HERE are many little points of etiquette and courteous observances which, if attended to, serve very materially to lighten the tedium and fatigue of travel, the non-observance of them being attended with proportionally disagreeable effects. No situation can be named where the difference between the well-bred and ill-bred of either sex is more marked than when they are upon a journey; and in this country, where all classes are thrown into contact in the various public conveyances, the annoyance of rude company can scarcely be exaggerated.

A gentleman, on entering a public carriage or omnibus, must never step before a lady, but stand aside until she enters, raising the hat slightly if she acknowledges his courtesy, as a true lady will, by a bow. He may offer to assist her if she appears to need it, even if she is a perfect stranger to him.

If a gentleman consents to act as escort to a lady, he must carefully fulfill all the requirements of that rather arduous position. If she meets him at a wharf

or depot, he must be a little before the hour for starting, to procure her ticket, check her baggage, and secure for her a pleasant seat.  He must never leave her
to stand in an office or upon a wharf whilst he attends
to her tickets and baggage; but, having seen her com-
fortably seated in a ladies' room or cabin, return for
those duties.  In arriving at a station, he must see her
seated in a hack before he attends to the trunks.

In a hotel, the gentleman must escort the lady to the
parlor before securing her room, but not detain her
afterwards.  However agreeable she may be, he may
be certain she is longing to rest after her journey, and
remove the travel stains from her face and dress.  He
must at once escort her to her room, ascertain what
hour it will be agreeable for her to take the next meal,
and meet her again in the parlor at that hour.

"Comparisons are odious," and to be continually
asserting that everything in the United States is vastly
superior to everything abroad is a mark of vulgarity.
If you really think there is nothing to be seen abroad
as good as you have at home, why, you are foolish
not to stay at home and enjoy the best.

If a train stop for refreshments, a gentleman may,
with perfect propriety, offer to escort a strange lady,
who is alone, to the refreshment-room, or to bring to
her any refreshments she may desire.  If she accepts

his offer, he must see that she is served with all that she desires before attending to his own wants.

Smoking in the presence of ladies is uncourteous, even if there is no law against it in the car, stage, or boat.

As regards the right to have the window up or down, the person who sits facing the engine has the command. Ladies, being present, should, of course, be consulted, no matter on which side they may be sitting, and their wish must be considered a final settlement of the question.

A gentleman who is traveling alone may offer little courtesies to strangers, and even to ladies, carefully maintaining a respectful manner, that may assure them they need not fear to encourage impertinence by accepting the proferred civilities.

## ETIQUETTE IN CHURCH.

IN visiting a church in which you have no pew of your own, wait in the vestibule until the sexton comes to you, and request him to show you to a seat. It is extremely rude to enter a pew without invitation if it is partially filled, or without permission if it is empty.

Always enter a church slowly and reverentially. **A** gentleman must remove his hat at the door, and never replace it until he is again in the vestibule.

Conform strictly to the forms of worship. If you are not familiar with them, rise, kneel, and sit as you see others do.

Never whisper to a companion in church.

Never bow to any friend while in the church itself. Greetings may be exchanged in the vestibule after service.

Gentlemen must pass up the aisle beside their lady companions until they reach the pew, then advance a few steps, open thc door, and stand aside until she has entered, then enter, and close the door again.

Never pay any attention to those around you, even if they are noisy or rude.

If you pass a book or a fan to a person in the same pew, or accept the same attention, it is not necessary to speak. A silent bow is all that etiquette requires.

If you have room in your own pew, and see a stranger enter, open the door and motion him to enter.

You may find the place and point it out to a stranger, who is unfamiliar with the service; but do so silently.

To come late to church is not only ill-bred, but

disrespectful. It is equally so to hurry away, or to commence preparations for departure, closing and putting away the books, and such preparations, before the service closes.

Never keep any one waiting if you are invited or have invited them to go to church.

It is ill-bred for gentlemen to congregate in the vestibule of a church and there chat familiarly, often commenting audibly upon the service or the congregation.

To show any disrespect to a form of worship that may be new or strange to you is rude in the extreme. To sneer at a form, while in the church using that form, is insulting and low bred.

---

## ETIQUETTE FOR PLACES OF AMUSE-MENT.

A GENTLEMAN who wishes to invite a young lady, who is not related to him, to visit any place of public amusement with him, must, the first time that he invites her, also invite another lady of the same family to accompany her.

It is a gentleman's duty to invite a lady long enough before the evening of the performance to be certain of securing pleasant seats, as it is but a poor compliment to take her where she will be uncomfortable, or where she can neither hear nor see.

Never assume an air of secrecy or mystery in a public place; and even if you have the right to do so, assume no lover-like airs. It is rude to converse loudly, especially during the performance; but a low tone is all that is necessary; not a whisper.

To appear to comment aside upon those near you is extremely ill-bred.

It is ill-bred to arrive late at any public entertainment, and looks as if you were not sufficiently master of your own time to be punctual.

In a theater, give your attention entirely to the stage when the curtain is up; to your companion when it is down.

If you speak to your companion during the performance, do so in a low tone, that you may not disturb those who are near you, and wish to hear the actors.

In entering a concert-room or the box of a theater, a gentleman should precede a lady, if there is not room to walk beside her, until they reach the seats, then hand her to the inner one, taking the outside one himself. In going out, if he cannot offer her his arm, he must again walk before her, until he reaches the lobby, and then offer her his arm.

Boisterous applause and loud laughter are ungentlemanly.

It is bad taste to distract your companion's interest from the performance, even if you find it dull yourself.

No gentleman should leave a lady alone for a moment in a public place of amusement.

In a picture-gallery, never stand conversing before the paintings in such a way as to interrupt the view of others. If you wish to converse, stand aside or take seats and do so.

It is an act of rudeness to join any party about to visit a place of amusement, or at one, unless urgently invited, and no one of taste will ever form a third.

Always enter a concert-hall or lecture-room as quietly as possible.

Never push violently through a crowd at a public place.

---

## TABLE ETIQUETTE.

IT is impossible for a gentleman to act with perfect ease and graceful manner at table when in company, at a hotel or any public place, unless he habitually pay attention to those minor points of etiquette, which form so distinctive a mark of perfectly good breeding.

Even when a person habitually eats alone, it is better to do so gracefully and with attention to the rules of etiquette, that habits of awkwardness may not be formed which it will be difficult to shake off when in company.

To make noises when eating, sucking soup with a gurgling sound, chewing meat noisily, swallowing as if with an effort, smacking the lips, or breathing heavily while masticating food, are all marks of low breeding.

It is a bad habit to put large pieces of food into the mouth.  If you are addressed suddenly with your mouth so filled, you are obliged to make an awkward pause before answering, or to run the risk of choking by swallowing the great mouthful too hastily.

Sit neither very near nor very far from the table.

To lean back in the chair is rude, and surely no gentleman would ever be guilty of tipping his chair at table.   Sit erect, not stiffly, but in an easy position.

Bread must always be broken, never cut, and certainly never bitten.

To eat very fast is inelegant; to eat very slowly bears an air of affectation.

A gentleman will always see that ladies are served before eating himself.

It is against all rules of etiquette to soak up gravy

with bread, to scrape up sauce with a spoon, or to take up bones with the fingers.

Never cross the knife and fork on a plate until you have finished eating.

Never hold your knife and fork erect in your hands at each side of your plate, when conversing at the table.

To blow soup to cool it, or to pour tea or coffee into a saucer for the same purpose, are acts of awkwardness never seen in polite society. Wait until they are cool enough to be pleasant.

Use the salt-spoon, butter-knife, and sugar-tongs even when you are alone.

If you want to cough, sneeze, or blow your nose, leave the table. If you have not time, turn away your head, and lean back in your chair.

To pass a plate with a knife or fork upon it, or a cup with a spoon in it, are acts of rudeness. Put your spoon in the saucer, and your knife and fork on the table, until you are served.

Never hurry away from the table as soon as you finish eating, if others remain to converse. If you are obliged to leave before a meal is finished or immediately after, ask to be excused for so doing, and apologize for the necessity.

At home, if you use a napkin-ring, fold your napkin

and replace it in the ring when you have done with it. If you are dining out, never fold your napkin, but place it beside your plate.

None but a clown would use the table-cloth for a napkin, pick his teeth with his fork, put his fingers in his plate, or wipe his face with his napkin.

If you are unfortunate enough to find anything disgusting in your food—a hair in the soup, a coal in the bread, a worm in the fruit, or a fly in your coffee—do not loudly exclaim, or disturb the appetite of others by mention of your mishap. Remove the disgusting object quietly, oa change your cup or plate without remark.

---

## THE GENTLEMAN'S TOILET.

THE first requisite of a gentleman's toilet is undoubtedly the bath, which should be as bracing as the constitution will allow, and used morning and evening in summer, and every day in winter. Only physiques of finest quality can endure, much more benefit by, a cold-water shock all the year round; and though physique is always improvable, great reformation must not be attempted rashly. Let the bath of from sixty to seventy degrees be freely indulged in by the strong, and even by the less robust, in summer time ; but in winter a temperature varying from eighty-five to ninety-five degrees is the safest. The flesh-brush should be vigorously applied to all parts of the body, after which the skin must be carefully dried with Turkish or huck-a-back towels.

The next thing to be done is to clean the teeth. This should be done with a good hard tooth-brush at least twice a day. Smokers should rinse the mouth immediately after smoking, and should be careful to keep the teeth scrupulously clean. The nails should also be kept exquisitely clean and short. Long nails are an abomination.

Our advice to those who shave is, like *Punch's* advice to those about to marry—" Don't." But it must by no means be understood that suffering the beard to grow is a process that obviates all trouble. The beard should be carefully and frequently washed, well trimmed, and well combed, and the hair and whiskers kept scrupulously clean by the help of clean, stiff hair-brushes, and soap and warm water. The style of the beard should be adapted to the form of the face; but any affectation in the cut of the beard and whiskers is very objectionable, and augurs unmitigated vanity in the wearer. Long hair is never indulged in except by painters and fiddlers.

Beau Brummell spent two hours in dressing; but a

gentleman can perform all the duties of his toilet to perfection in less than half that time.

A gentleman should always be so well dressed that his dress shall never be remarked at all. Does this sound like an enigma? It is not meant for one. It only implies that perfect simplicity is perfect elegance, and that the true test of dress in the toilet of a gentleman is its entire harmony, unobtrusiveness, and becomingness.

A man whose dress is appropriate, neat and clean, will always look like a gentleman; but to dress appropriately, one must have a varied wardrobe. This should not, on the average, cost more than a tenth part of his income. No man can afford more than a tenth of his income for dress.

The author of "Pelham" has aptly said that "a gentleman's coat shonld not fit too well." To be fitted too well is to look.like a tailor's dummy.

For evening parties, dinner parties and balls, wear a black dress coat, black trousers, black silk or cloth vest, thin patent-leather boots, a white cravat, and white kid gloves. Abjure all fopperies, such as white silk linings, silk collars, etc.; above all, the shirt-front should be plain. At small, unceremonious parties, gloves are not necessary; but, when worn, they should be new and fit well. A man's jewelry should be of the best and simplest description. False jewelry, like every other form of falsehood and pretence, is unmitigated vulgarity.

Elaborate studs and sleeve-links are all foppish and vulgar. A set of good studs, a gold watch and guard, and one handsome ring, are as many ornaments as a gentleman can wear with propriety.

Lastly, a man's jewelry should always have some use, and not like a lady's, be worn for ornament only.

Colored shirts may be worn in the morning; but they should be small in pattern and quiet in color. Fancy cloths of conspicuous patterns are exceedingly objectionable. The hat should always be black; and caps and straw hats are only admissible in summer.

A man's clothes should always be well brushed, and never threadbare or shabby. No gentleman can afford to wear shabby clothes.

For the country, or the foreign tour, a gentleman will select a costume of some light woolen material, flannel shirts, thick boots, and everything to correspond.

There are three things one should consult in the matter of dress if one would always appear like a gentleman—viz., expense, comfort, and society. If there is one thing in this world about which we can entertain any degree of moral certainty, it is that we must pay our tailor's bills. If, therefore, our means are disproportionate to our wants, we must remember the old proverb, " Cut your coat according to your cloth," and dress as well as you possibly can upon little money.

---

## MISCELLANEOUS.

A GENTLEMAN must always hand a lady a chair, open the door for her to pass in or out, remove anything that may be in her way, and pick up anything she may drop, even if she is an entire stranger to him.

A gentleman will never look over the shoulder of another who is either reading or writing.

No gentleman will ever be guilty of personality in conversation. No wit, however keen; no sarcasm, however humorous, can make personal remarks anything but rude and vulgar.

A gentleman, in passing a lady where he must stand aside to give her space, must always remove his hat, and incline his head slightly.

It is a mark of low breeding to fidget either with the hands or feet; to play with the watch-chain, toss the gloves, suck the head of a cane or handle of a parasol, or to fuss with a collar or necktie.

To swing the foot, or tap monotonously with the feet, to drum with the fingers on a table or window, are all breaches of etiquette.

It is ill-bred to speak of persons with whom you are but slightly acquainted, by their first name.

Mysterious allusions are rude.

Flattery is a breach of etiquette. Johnson says: "Of all wild beasts, preserve me from a tyrant; and of all tame, a flatterer."

No gentleman may ever break an engagement, whether it be one of business or pleasure, with a lady, or with another gentleman. To break an engagement with a lady is almost certain to give lasting offence, and with good cause.

Irritability is a breach of good manners. Watts says: "To be angry about trifles is mean and childish; to rage and be furious is brutish; and to maintain perpetual wrath is akin to the practice and temper of fiends; but to prevent and suppress rising resentment is wise and glorious, is manly and divine."

Nothing marks a gentleman more truly than a strict punctuality. To keep another waiting is a breach of etiquette, as well as often a positive unkindness.

To answer a civil question rudely, or even impatiently, is a gross breach of etiquette. Even if it inconveniences you or interrupts you, it will take no longer to answer kindly or politely than to wound or offend by crustiness.

No gentleman may ever refuse an apology. No matter how great the offence, how deep the resentment, an apology can never be rejected. It may not again revive friendship; but it must prevent quarreling.

An invalid, an elderly person, or a lady, must be given the most comfortable chair in the room, must be allowed to select the light and temperature, and no true lady or gentleman will ever object to the exercise of the privilege.

To assume a lazy, lounging attitude in company is unmannerly. If any one is too weak or too ill to sit up and assume a proper position, he had better stay at home until he is stronger or in better health.

Never rise to take leave in the midst of an interesting conversation; wait until there is a pause, and then withdraw, with as little disturbance as possible.

It is proper, before taking a place at table, to say "Good morning," or "Good evening," to those in the room before you, and especially to those who preside over the meal.

It is a breach of etiquette to go into company with the breath tainted by eating onions, garlic, cheese, or any other strong-scented food.

**MISCELLANEOUS.** 399

It is a breach of etiquette for a gentleman to enter a lady's presence smelling of tobacco or wine.

To notice, by look or word, any deformity, any scar or misfortune to the face or figure of a friend, is not only a breach of etiquette of the grossest kind, but is a want of humanity and good feeling as well.

It is a breach of etiquette to lean heavily upon a table; and also to tip a chair to and fro when you are talking; and you will be justly punished if you find yourself sprawling on the floor with the chair on top of you.

The man who will insult his inferiors is a boor at heart, however polished he may appear amongst his equals, or however deferential to his superiors.

To imitate the manners, voice, attitude, or gestures of great men were a folly almost too absurd to mention if it were not so common. Many persons, from a real or fancied personal resemblance to some celebrity, will ape their manners also, as if mere appearance would make them equally distinguished.

" The scholar, without good breeding, is a pedant; the philosopher, a cynic; the soldier, a brute; and every man disagreeable," says Chesterfield.

Bishop Beveridge says: " Never speak of a man's virtues before his face, nor of his faults behind his back."

" In private, watch your thoughts; in your family, watch your temper; in society, watch your tongue."

" To arrive at the heart of true courtesy," says a modern writer, " separate the old English titles for the well-bred; they were the *gentle*-man and *gentle*-woman."

It is better to live alone than in low company. If you cannot keep good company, keep none.

Sterne thus defines courtship: " True courtship consists in a number of quiet, gentlemanly attentions; not so pointed as to alarm, not so vague as to be misunderstood."

It is a breach of etiquette to enter a room noisily, slamming the door, or stamping heavily upon the floor.

Spitting is as vulgar as it is disgusting.

It is ill-bred to refuse the last piece on the plate or dish, if it is offered to you, as it implies a fear that there is no more in the pantry.

To yawn, blow the nose loudly, suck or pick the teeth, or clean the nails in company, are breaches of etiquette.

Gentlemen should never stand upon the hearthrug with their backs to the fire, either in a friend's house or their own.